✳ LADIES OF THE LIGHTS ✳

Big Sable Point was the tallest lighthouse at which Michigan women served. Elsea Hyde and Sarah Caswell assisted their husbands in the 112-foot tower. *Photo courtesy of the Archives of Michigan*

Ladies of the Lights

Michigan Women in the U.S. Lighthouse Service

Patricia Majher

THE UNIVERSITY OF MICHIGAN PRESS
Ann Arbor

2013   2012   2011   2010   4   3   2

A CIP catalog record for this book is available from the British Library.

Library of Congress Cataloging-in-Publication Data

Majher, Patricia.
    Ladies of the lights : Michigan women in the U.S. Lighthouse
Service / Patricia Majher.
        p.   cm.
    Includes bibliographical references and index.
    ISBN 978-0-472-07143-2 (cloth : acid-free paper) — ISBN 978-0-
472-05143-4 (pbk. : acid-free paper)
        1. Women lighthouse keepers—Michigan—History.   2. Women
lighthouse keepers—Michigan—Biography.   3. Lighthouses—Michigan—
History.   4. Lighthouse keepers—Michigan—History.   5. Lighthouse
keepers—Michigan—Biography.   6. Women lighthouse keepers—United
States—History.   7. Women lighthouse keepers—United States—
Biography.   8. United States. Bureau of Light-Houses.   I. Title.
VK1024.M5M35   2010
386'.85508209774—dc22   2010017702

    ISBN13: 978-0-472-02801-6 (electronic)

To my husband

BRAD CHARTIER

whose selfless support

makes all things possible

✳ CONTENTS ✳

❋ ACKNOWLEDGMENTS ❋

I wish to thank the Michigan Women's Historical Center and Hall of Fame for providing the opportunity to delve into such a fascinating topic in the process of developing the "Ladies of the Lights: Michigan Women in the U.S. Lighthouse Service" exhibit. The discovery of an original copy of *A Child of the Sea; and Life among the Mormons*—the memoir of Michigan keeper Elizabeth Van Riper Williams—in the Historical Center's library was the first step on my journey of discovery that resulted in the book you now hold in your hands.

Much of my research time was spent in the stacks of the Library of Michigan, which has an extensive collection of lighthouse books of state and national interest. I am also indebted to the following archivists, curators, historians, and librarians who provided invaluable resources along the way: Alicia Allen, Maud Preston Palenske Memorial Library; Christina Hirn Arseneau, Heritage Museum and Cultural Center of St. Joseph; Ron Bloomfield, Bay County Historical Society; Cathi Bulone Campbell, Sanilac County Historic Village and Museum; Katheryn Carrier, Traverse Area District Library; Bill Cashman, Beaver Island Historical Society; Dennis Copeland, Monterey (California) Public Library; Wallace Hayden, Bacon Memorial District Library; Judith Kimball, Presque Isle Township Museum Society; Jerry Lenz, Keweenaw County Historical Society; Carol Lewis, Old Mission Peninsula Historical Society; Sean Ley, Great Lakes Shipwreck Historical Society; Vicki Mann, Peter White Public Library; Julie Meyerle, Archives of Michigan; Malgosia Myc, Bentley Historical Library/University of Michigan; Jim Orr and Kathy

Steiner, Benson Ford Research Center/The Henry Ford; Sandy Planisek, Great Lakes Lighthouse Keepers Association; Davonne Rogers, Presque Isle District Library; Stephen Saks, New York Public Library; Peg Siciliano, Traverse Area Historical Society/Grand Traverse Heritage Center; Patricia Simons, Ontonagon County Historical Museum; Holly Smith, Crane Hill Publishers; and Stefanie Staley, Grand Traverse Lighthouse Museum.

Chief among the individuals who helped me in my quest for information was Dianna Stampfler, founder of Promote Michigan, whose love affair with lighthouses prompted her to develop a series of lectures on female lighthouse keepers of the Great Lakes as well as ghost stories associated with Michigan lights. She shared her resources selflessly with me and was the person who introduced me to Michigan's last lady lighthouse keeper: Frances Wuori Johnson (now Marshall). Dianna was also kind enough to let me borrow the phrase that served as a title for both my exhibit and this book.

Terry Pepper, executive director of the Great Lakes Lighthouse Keepers Association, lent his encyclopedic knowledge of Michigan lights to my two projects and served as fact-checker extraordinaire. His personal website, "Seeing the Light: Lighthouses of the Western Great Lakes" at www.terrypepper.com—which incorporates a treasure trove of keeper data compiled by Thomas and Phyllis Tag—is rightfully regarded as the premier online resource on this subject.

I was also privileged to communicate with the descendants of several female lighthouse keepers and keepers' wives, including Richard Campbell (Edna Campbell); Mary Lou Dacey (Anna and Mary Garraty); Chris Shanley-Dillman (Anastasia Truckey); Marcia Franz (Mary Ann Wheatley); Cindy Krueger and Jeff Shook (Catherine Shook); Jeremiah Mason (Mary Corgan); Holly Nolan (Frances Marshall); Arthur Schlichting (Grace Holmes); and Jack Sheridan (Julia Sheridan), who were generous in sharing images and information about their accomplished ancestors.

And last, but certainly not least, Frances Marshall deserves my special thanks for welcoming me into her home, sharing her personal history as a keeper, and serving as the last living link to the more than fifty women we proudly call Michigan's Ladies of the Lights.

✴ LADIES OF THE LIGHTS ✴

Introduction

Lighthouse keeping in the nineteenth and early twentieth centuries was a rugged life filled with long hours and hard work punctuated by periods of real peril. Not a profession for the fainthearted, it was thought by many to be unsuitable employment for the "fairer sex."

But more than fifty women in Michigan proved the naysayers wrong.

Acting as both assistants and full-fledged keepers, these women served the sailing community with distinction for more than a hundred years—often juggling their official duties with the demands of raising their families. Several of these women even died while in the service.

But where are their stories told? In history books, in the classroom, on TV, or in the movies? The sad truth is that—with the exception of a book chapter here and there—the contributions of Michigan's "Ladies of the Lights" have almost been lost to time.

The inspiration for this book was Kathy Mason's cover story for the September/October 2003 issue of *Michigan History* magazine. Entitled "Mystery at Sand Point Lighthouse," it attempted to answer questions surrounding the death of keeper Mary Terry, whose body was consumed by a terrible fire that struck her Escanaba lighthouse in 1886. More intriguing than the mystery of "whodunnit," though, was the inclusion in the article of a table of names of forty-nine other women who had served their country (as lighthouse keeping was a federal job) and their state in this unique profession.

Besides names, the table also listed the lights these women

Historians believe this may be the only known photograph of Sand Point (Escanaba) keeper Mary Terry, who died in a suspicious fire at the lighthouse in 1886. *Photo courtesy of the New York Public Library, Robert N. Dennis Collection of Stereoscopic Views*

kept—all over lakes Huron, Michigan, and Superior as well as on the Detroit River—and the years during which they served. Some stayed for only a year or less; were they just placeholders until a permanent keeper could be found? And several women were employed between the years 1861 and 1865, begging the question: Were they filling in for a husband called away to war?

And what about the woman who was posted at two lights on Lake Michigan—Beaver Island Harbor and Little Traverse—for a combined total of forty-one years? What was her story? Can we assume that she loved her work, or she never would have stayed so long?

If last names are any indication, it also appeared that some of the women in the keepers' list might have been related and, if so, in what way?

In short, more questions were raised than answered by the *Michigan History* article. But they were good questions meriting more research.

The opportunity to engage in that research came in 2007, when this book's author was hired as the assistant director/curator for the Michigan Women's Historical Center and Hall of Fame in Lansing. The Historical Center houses the only museum in the state dedicated to women's history. And one of the first responsibilities of the new curator was to develop an exhibit to place in the museum's changing gallery.

It didn't take long to zero in on a subject: Michigan's female lighthouse keepers. The topic of lighthouses has universal appeal in Michigan, home of the greatest concentration of lights in the United States. And lighthouse *keepers*—illustrated in our imaginations by a solitary figure surveying the seas from a lofty tower—are viewed as equally romantic. Layer on top of that the prospect of a female face and you have the foundation of an intriguing educational display.

The exhibit was quite popular—more so than any other previously launched by the institution. And it continues to be enjoyed by new audiences each year as it circulates among cultural institutions—museums, libraries, and schools—in the state.

This book was intended to present the themes of the original exhibit—e.g., how did female keepers get appointed to these jobs? how did they tend a light and a family at the same time? were they treated differently from men?—and to expand on the discussion of its themes. Those who have seen the exhibit will enjoy reading more about the trials and triumphs of these amazing Michigan women. Those who haven't seen the exhibit will be able to pick up the story of Michigan's Ladies of the Lights from the very beginning, when a widow stranded in the Michigan wilderness of the 1840s with eight children to feed decides she can, indeed she must, take up where her late keeper husband left off: serving the sailors of the state until the sun rises again.

✳ A Note about the Lighthouse Service ✳

The history of lighthouse administration in the United States began in colonial times, when England's indifference forced colonial governments to shoulder the responsibility of making coastal waters safe to sail. In 1789, eight years after the Revolutionary War ended, the Congress of the United States created the Lighthouse Establishment to administer the growing inventory of aids to navigation.

Over a period of 150 years, the Lighthouse Establishment was variously known as the Lighthouse Board, the Bureau of Lighthouses, and the Lighthouse Service. (To prevent confusion, the phrase "Lighthouse Service" is used throughout this book.)

In 1939, the Lighthouse Service was transferred to and assimilated into the U.S. Coast Guard.

✳ CHAPTER ONE ✳

Female Lighthouse Keepers: A Brief History

Mary Louise and J. Candace Clifford have written the foremost reference work about female lighthouse keepers in the United States. But a condensed version of that history may be useful to readers embarking on this book.

America's First Female Keeper

The story begins in the early eighteenth century, with the illumination of the inaugural "aid to navigation" in U.S. waters: Little Brewster Island lighthouse in Boston Harbor. First lit in 1716, it was manned—literally—by a fellow known as George Worthylake.[1] Ten more lights were constructed up and down the East Coast, and nearly sixty years would pass before the first *female* keeper in the United States would be appointed. Her name was Hannah Thomas.

Initially serving as assistant, Hannah took full responsibility for the Gurnet Point lights at the entrance to Plymouth Bay (Massachusetts) when her keeper husband John left to fight in the colonial army in 1775. He never returned to his home, having died of smallpox in Canada. In his stead, Hannah assumed the difficult task of maintaining not one but two lanterns on the site, even surviving a skirmish between a British ship and a local militia that was guarding the lights. Her son succeeded her as keeper in 1790.[2]

※ The World's First Female Keepers Were Irish Nuns ※

Lighthouse expert Francis Ross Holland believed that the world's first female keeper likely served in Ireland.[3] And the website of the Commissioners of Irish Lights confirms that "Youghal lighthouse [on the southern coast of Ireland] was built in 1190 and was placed under the care of the nuns of [nearby] St. Anne's convent."[4] The women there were said to have used torches to guide vessels into the harbor, continuing as keepers until the convent was dissolved in 1542.

The Great Lakes' First

According to lighthouse historian Francis Ross Holland, the earliest lighthouses on the Great Lakes were lit at Presque Isle, Pennsylvania, and Buffalo, New York, in 1819.[5] Two years later, the first tower in Ohio was erected on the tip of Marblehead Peninsula at the narrow entrance to Sandusky Bay. Benajah Wolcott was appointed keeper there and served admirably until a cholera epidemic took his life in 1832. His widow, Rachel Wolcott, became the first Lady of the Light in the region when she was named by the federal government as his replacement.

For two years, Rachel lit the wicks of thirteen whale-oil lamps each night as a signal to passing ships. She then stepped down so that her second husband might take the top job; he kept the light for an additional ten years. All in all, Rachel Wolcott van Benschoten devoted twenty-two years of her life to Marblehead.[6]

Michigan's First

In Michigan, the earliest lighthouse was established at Fort Gratiot (Port Huron) in 1825.[7] But the state's first female keeper—Catherine Shook of Pointe aux Barques—didn't assume her position until

Michigan's last Lady of the Light, Frances Wuori Johnson, was also the only one to serve during the Coast Guard era. *Photo courtesy of Frances Marshall*

twenty-four years later.[8] Poor health and the demands of tending a light *and* a family of eight prompted her to resign her post in 1851. (More detail on Catherine Shook's life may be found in chapter 11.)

Three years passed before a second Michigan woman appeared in the records of the U.S. Lighthouse Service: Mrs. Charles O'Malley at Bois Blanc Island.[9] And just ten more of the state's women were on the books up until 1869 despite efforts by federal administrators to compensate keepers' widows with gainful employment.[10]

The 1870s were the high-water mark for women in the service, both in the nation and in Michigan.[11] During that decade, twenty-two were employed at important lights on lakes Huron, Michigan, and Superior and on the Detroit River. By the 1880s, however, the national population of women keepers began to drop. In Michigan, that number dipped to sixteen and, in the 1890s, to ten.

After 1920, only three women still maintained lights in Michigan; changing technology and the assumption of the Lighthouse Service into the all-male U.S. Coast Guard in 1939 are generally regarded as the reasons. When Frances Wuori Johnson of the White River light resigned her post in 1954, her action marked the official end of the 105-year history of female lighthouse keepers in the state.

CHAPTER TWO

Michigan: Home to the Most Female Keepers

Michigan's leadership role in U.S. lighthouse history is undeniable; for one thing, it's the state in which the *most lighthouses* were erected. And more than 120 remain there, as compared to five hundred total in the rest of the nation.[1]

By extension, Michigan also recorded the *most keepers* in the Lighthouse Service and earned another distinction as well: It was home to the *most female keepers*. Twenty-seven of the state's women served as principal keepers out of approximately 140 across the country. Another twenty-five Michigan women were appointed assistant keepers.[2]

Do sheer numbers of lighthouses and keepers dictate that Michigan should also lead in this third category? "That would be a safe assumption," noted J. Candace Clifford, who coauthored *Women Who Kept the Lights*, the first book to focus on women in the Lighthouse Service.[3] Gladys Beckwith, founder of the Michigan Women's Historical Center and Hall of Fame, suggests a second possibility: "At the same time Michigan women were making a name for themselves in the service, their sisters around the state were making history as national leaders in the fight to win women the right to vote and assume other rights in our society."

"It comes as no surprise to me," she added, "that Michigan women rose to the challenges of lighthouse keeping with the same vigor and resolve."[4]

By all accounts of the period, Michigan's female keepers *were* vigorous women who took their profession very seriously. While the

Mary Corgan, who assisted her husband James at Gull Rock and Manitou Island, was one of only three Michigan women who served at more than one lighthouse. *Photo courtesy of the Keweenaw National Historical Park*

majority succeeded their husbands in the job, several secured appointments on their own: a rare accomplishment for women in the service.

Reports of bad behavior were rare among Michigan's Ladies of the Lights. And, like their national counterparts, they stayed longer at each posting and committed to longer careers than did men—some into their sixties and seventies.[5]

Michigan women bravely faced the most challenging assignments, with many serving at remote stations such as Au Sable Point. Located along the southern shore of Lake Superior, the lighthouse was twelve miles away from the nearest village along a narrow path hugging the base of steep sand dunes. On windy days, the trail was virtually impassable due to crashing waves. And, though its lamp was first lit in 1874, no road connected the lighthouse to civilization until 1928. To say it was a difficult posting for families would be an understatement. The Northern Michigan University Center for Upper Peninsula Studies noted that wintertime seclusion was partly to blame for the deaths of one keeper's son and daughter.[6]

Gull Rock was the temporary home of three female keepers: the most of any posting in Michigan. *Photo courtesy of the Archives of Michigan*

✳ Was Gull Rock Michigan's Most Female-Friendly Lighthouse? ✳

Gull Rock lighthouse, situated in Lake Superior east of the tip of the Keweenaw Peninsula, had three female keepers in its history: the most of any individual lighthouse in Michigan. Lighthouse historian Terry Pepper opined that the light station's location—on a rocky island, with no soil to speak of—inspired the service to name these women assistants to their keeper husbands to compensate for such a confining post.[7]

The weather played a part in the death of at least one of the state's female keepers, who drowned when a boat she was riding in capsized in Lake Michigan. Another died in a suspicious fire that struck her wooden lighthouse one fateful night in 1886.

Despite the dangers of the job and its physical demands, Michigan's female keepers stayed the course for more than a hundred years—only leaving the Lighthouse Service when its administration (and, later, that of the Coast Guard) discouraged requests for continued employment.

The lives of these fifty-two women have not been as well documented as those of their male counterparts. But, thanks to records preserved in the National Archives as well as in county histories, contemporary news accounts, genealogies, and one keeper's autobiography, we can answer some basic questions about Michigan's Ladies of the Lights.

CHAPTER THREE

Typical Duties of a Lighthouse Keeper

To fully appreciate the challenges that women faced in the light keeping profession, you must first understand what any keeper or assistant keeper was expected to do. The following excerpt from an 1835 document issued by the superintendent of lighthouses details just a few of those responsibilities:

1. You are to light the lamps every evening at sun-setting, and keep them continually burning bright and clear till sun-rising.
2. You are to be careful that the lamps, reflectors, and lanterns [the glass-enclosed room at the top of a tower] are constantly kept clean, and in order; and particularly to be careful that no lamps, wood, or candles be left burning anywhere so as to endanger fire.
3. In order to maintain the greatest degree of light during the night, the wicks are to be trimmed every four hours, taking care that they are exactly even on top.
4. You are to keep an exact account of the quantity of oil received from time to time; the number of gallons, quarts, gills, [etc.] consumed each night, and deliver a copy of the same to the superintendent every three months. . . .[1]

Michigan's earliest lady lighthouse keepers worked with Lewis lamps: an array of multiple oil-burning fixtures, each outfitted with a reflector and lens to magnify and focus the light out over the water.[2] The

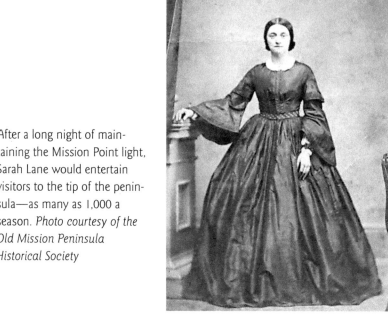

After a long night of maintaining the Mission Point light, Sarah Lane would entertain visitors to the tip of the peninsula—as many as 1,000 a season. *Photo courtesy of the Old Mission Peninsula Historical Society*

Lewis lamps had their flaws—the reflectors warped out of shape and shed their reflective coating, while the entire assembly sooted up very quickly—so they were replaced starting in 1852 with a French invention. The large and intricately designed Fresnel lenses magnified light to such a degree that one oil-burning lamp placed inside could do the work of many.[3]

Although Fresnel lenses greatly improved safety on the seas (and Great Lakes), they did relatively little to simplify the jobs of keepers and assistants, who still had to take shifts to ensure that their lamps stayed lit from sundown to sunup and that the clockwork-like mechanisms that rotated later lenses stayed in motion.

Keeping a lamp lit when the wind was gusting or a storm was raging could prove quite challenging. A newspaper reporter described Mission Point keeper Sarah Lane's response to bad weather in this way:

On a windy night, there is danger of [the lamp] smoking or going down, and the colder the weather and worse the storm, the

14

Compare this photograph of Julia Sheridan, dated 1866, to that on page 28. Taken only 11 years apart, the two images demonstrate how hard a life lighthouse keeping could be. *Photo courtesy of Jack Sheridan*

oftener must Mrs. Lane make her weary trips to the top of the tower to guard against trouble. On frosty nights, the [lantern window] panes must be frequently wiped with glycerin to keep them clear.[4]

In foggy weather, early keepers were also responsible for stoking the coal-burning boilers that powered their fog signals—sometimes day and night. In 1887, a particularly inclement year, Patrick and Catharine McGuire kept their Marquette Harbor signal screaming for 697 hours: a light station record.[5]

At daybreak, keepers would extinguish their lamps, close the curtains in the lantern, and turn their attention toward record keeping—for example, recording the weather, ship sightings, and other details of the day in a logbook—and maintaining the light station's structures and equipment. This was a critical part of the job, as stations were inspected periodically by federal officials who had the power to penalize and even remove errant keepers.[6]

Typical tower chores included refilling the lamp with oil (until the electrification of lighthouses started in the 1920s); polishing the lighthouse glass and brass; washing the windows of the lantern; and scrubbing the tower floors and steps. The keeper's residence also had to be kept clean and uncluttered. Meals needed to be cooked and laundry done. And, if the light station was blessed with the right kind of soil to sustain a garden, there were planting, weeding, and harvesting chores to do. Some keepers even raised livestock.

If that weren't enough, keepers were additionally directed by the Lighthouse Service to "treat with civility and attention such strangers as may visit the light-house under your charge."[7]

Like their male counterparts, female keepers no doubt engaged family members in the execution of some of these tasks to lighten the load. Still, the primary responsibilities fell on their shoulders. That burden is evident in the faces of the few Ladies of the Lights for whom "before keeping" and "after keeping" photographs exist.

During the shipping season on the Great Lakes—then running between May and November—keepers were expected to stay at their posts every day. The nineteenth-century rules about leaving were very specific: "You will not absent yourself from the light-house at any time without first obtaining the consent of the Superintendent, unless the occasion be so sudden and urgent as not to admit of an application to

---

✳ Nolen Suffers the Loss of Two Children ✳

Female keepers also acted as "Dr. Mom," treating the injuries and illnesses of their families at the light station. But Alice Nolen, assistant at Gull Rock light, could do nothing to save her two oldest children during an epidemic of scarlet fever that occurred while they wintered on the mainland in Calumet. Aged three and seven, the girl and boy both died during the winter of 1900. Wrote their father, John, in his logbook: "O! How we long for the touch of those little vanished hands—and the voices we loved that are still."[8]

that officer; in which case, by leaving a suitable substitute, you may be absent for twenty-four hours."[9] In the twentieth century, regulations were a little more relaxed, especially at minor stations. Noted Frances Wuori Johnson, a keeper at the electrified White River light in the 1940s and 1950s: "I did go down [to my parents' home in Pontiac] once and visited for about three days. I had [a neighbor] watch the light for me. I gave her my mother's phone number. Everything worked out okay. That was the only time I was ever gone."[10]

CHAPTER FOUR

How Did Women Get Appointed to Keeper Positions?

The wives (and sometimes daughters) of keepers had little trouble being named *assistant* keepers in the Lighthouse Service; if their relatives requested the appointment, it was generally granted. But getting a woman named the *principal* keeper at a light? That was another thing altogether.

Until 1896, when lighthouse keepers became civil servants, principal keepers acquired their positions by federal appointment on the recommendation of the local collector of customs. As most customs officials were male, they tended to suggest keeper candidates who were male. Appointments were also granted as favors to veterans of military service or to members of the prevailing political party—again tilting the odds in favor of men.[1]

Stephen Pleasonton, the federal official responsible for the Lighthouse Service from 1820 to 1852, did what he could to change this system. In an 1851 letter to his superior, Secretary of the Treasury Thomas Corwin, Pleasonton wrote:

> It must be apparent to all who reflect upon the subject, that I have had much inconvenience and difficulty to encounter from the frequent changes incidental to our form of government, in the [politically appointed] keepers, who for a time do not understand the management of their lamps, and consequently keep bad lights and waste much oil. So necessary is it that the lights should be in the hands of experienced keepers, that I [do], in order to effect that object as far as possible, recommend,

on the death of a keeper, that his widow, if steady and respectable, should be appointed to succeed him.[2]

Pleasonton's suggestion appears to have been taken seriously; approximately thirty widows were named keepers nationwide in the 1850s and nearly fifty by the 1870s.[3]

Michigan women who benefited from this recommendation included Mary Vreeland succeeding Michael Vreeland at the Gibraltar lighthouse, Slatira Carlton succeeding Monroe Carlton at St. Joseph, and Elizabeth Van Riper (later Williams) succeeding Clement Van Riper at Beaver Island Harbor. (It should be noted, however, that

Patrick Garraty was granted the right to hire his wife Mary as assistant keeper at New Presque Isle light, an arrangement that supplemented the family income for 10 years. *Photo courtesy of the Presque Isle Township Museum Society*

Mary Ann Wheatley was unique in that she did not succeed her deceased husband at his light. Her appointment was a day's sail away on the other side of the Keweenaw Peninsula. *Photo courtesy of Marcia Franz*

Williams's professionalism on Beaver Island earned her next appointment at Little Traverse light on her own merits.)

Though a widow of a lighthouse keeper, Mary Ann Wheatley did not succeed her husband, William, at his last posting: Marquette Harbor. Instead, three weeks after his drowned body was found near the mouth of the Little Garlic River, Mary was appointed keeper at Eagle Harbor Range lights and remained there for seven years.[4]

Another way that women could gain a position as principal keeper was if their keeper husbands enlisted for military service. This

Anastasia Truckey was a wife and mother living in Detroit shortly before she took on the responsibility of keeping the Marquette Harbor light, which protected iron ore shipments bound for Northern factories during the Civil War. *Photo courtesy of Chris Shanley-Dillman*

was the case for Anastasia Truckey, who maintained the light in Marquette Harbor for three years after her husband, Nelson Truckey, helped form Company B, 27th Infantry Regiment, Michigan Volunteers, and left for parts south to fight in the Civil War.[5] (A historical novel titled *Finding My Light*, written by a descendant of the Truckeys, weaves facts about Anastasia's keeping career and her children with a fictional subplot involving a young man who may or may not be a Confederate spy.)

✳ Johnson Fights for the Right to Serve ✳

Bucking both the widow and wartime trends, White River assistant Frances Wuori Johnson earned her keeper job the old-fashioned way: She lobbied for it. After she and keeper Leo Wuori divorced and resigned from their duties, she had second thoughts about leaving the profession. Frances then wrote to the Coast Guard, calling attention to her accomplishments as an assistant, and in 1949 she successfully secured the senior position back at her old light.[6]

The Spanish–American War, a military conflict that took place between April and August 1898, also attracted the interest of many able-bodied keepers. After the Lighthouse Service granted permission for its male employees to enlist in the war effort, wives like Jennie Beamer at Big Bay Point and Lucy Gramer at Ecorse Range filled in for them while they were away—temporarily earning the men's titles and pay.[7]

CHAPTER FIVE

What Drew Women to This Work?

It's a sad fact, but true: Most women became lighthouse keepers to provide for themselves and their children after the death of a keeper husband.[1] And some were relatives of keepers who just fell naturally into the profession. One example of this was Caroline Warner—an assistant keeper for ten years at the St. Clair Flats South Channel Range lights—who was the daughter-in-law, sister-in-law, wife, and mother of keepers.[2] Anna Garraty—who served at Presque Isle Harbor—also had lighthouse keeping in her blood. Her parents were both keepers and passed the profession along to Anna and three of her siblings.[3]

For still others, the lure was almost indescribable. Elizabeth Van Riper Williams spoke of it this way in her memoir, *A Child of the Sea; and Life among the Mormons*:

> From the first the work had a fascination for me. I loved the water, having always been near it, and I loved to stand in the tower and watch the great rolling waves chasing and tumbling in upon the shore. It was hard to tell when it was loveliest. Whether in its quiet moods or in a raging foam.[4]

Money may also have been a motivation for some women. Lighthouse keeping was one of the few positions at which women could earn as much as men; even Michigan's first female keeper, Catherine Shook, made the same salary—$300 a year—as her male predecessor and successor.[5] What's more, women's job opportunities in the late

Daughter Anna Garraty (pictured here) and mother Mary Garraty are the only Michigan female keepers known to have been related. *Photo courtesy of the Presque Isle Township Museum Society*

Elizabeth Van Riper Williams is the only Lady of the Light to have written an autobiography. In it, she described her life on the Great Lakes, contact with American Indians, and the Mormon colony on Beaver Island. *Photo courtesy of the Beaver Island Historical Society*

✳ Pentwater Keeper Was Kicked Out of Her Job ✳

Though most keepers appreciated the steady employment the service provided, the isolation and monotony of the work drove others to distraction—or worse. After performing ably for eight years following the death of her husband, the keeper of the Pentwater Pier light started acting in an unprofessional manner. The Naval Secretary of the Lighthouse Board wrote to his superior that "Mrs. Annie McGuire has been reported...for drunkenness and irregular habits."[6] These were serious charges, and the district inspector recommended McGuire's removal. Acting swiftly to ensure the safety of Lake Michigan mariners, the board dismissed her eight days later. And that appeared to be the end of her lighthouse-keeping career.

---

nineteenth and early twentieth centuries were frequently limited to the home (housekeeper or cook) or to industry (mill and factory jobs). Being your own boss or a valued assistant to the boss in a field that was important to your state and the nation? That had some status associated with it.

Despite the practical advantages of a career in the Lighthouse Service, few females took up the challenge. And some who did paid a painful price. Two lost their lives—one by drowning, one by fire—on the job. Some, like Alice Nolen, buried children.[7] But, in terms of sheer numbers, Elizabeth Van Riper Williams suffered the greatest losses among Michigan women: losing her first husband to a watery death as well as two brothers and three nephews.[8]

CHAPTER SIX

What Special Hardships Did Women Face?

Aside from the challenge of giving birth at remote postings—far from midwives and medical doctors—Michigan women in the Lighthouse Service faced the same hardships as men. Among the most difficult challenges to fight was the feeling of isolation.

Some lighthouses were built in the most remote places. M. A. Stevens bravely took on Michigan's most distant assignment when she assisted her husband, William Stevens, at the Menagerie Island (Isle Royale) lighthouse fifty miles out in Lake Superior. Far from friends and family, they set up their household and lit the lamps for the first time on October 19, 1875. They had only seven days to experience the solitude of the light station before an epic storm arose. William's entry in the light station logbook described it in this way:

✳ Truckey Saves a Visiting Relative from Reprisal ✳

While her husband was off fighting in the Civil War, keeper Anastasia Truckey developed a close relationship with a band of American Indians who lived near her Marquette Harbor lighthouse. Family legend notes they even called her "mother of the light." That relationship proved invaluable, apparently, when one of her relatives treated an Indian with disrespect, and Truckey had to intercede on his behalf. "He [the relative] was allowed to keep his hair," was how Truckey family historian Robert Shanley described it.[1]

M. A. Stevens served as assistant keeper at Menagerie Island lighthouse: the northernmost beacon in Michigan waters that employed a woman. *Photo courtesy of the Archives of Michigan*

"Damp and cloudy. The east northeast gale increased almost to hurricane. At 6 a.m., the sea went clear over [the 61-foot] tower...and broke the window sashes on south side of house. Washed away everything loose, lumber, wood, rocks off the island."[2]

Bad weather also took its toll on keepers at Au Sable Point. Within three weeks of her arrival at the light station, Mary Beedon experienced a fearsome winter storm that destroyed fifty nearby trees and caused her husband, Napoleon Beedon, to fear that "the lighthouse and tower would be blown down as they shook like a leaf."[3] Mary and Gus Gigandet, who came to the same light in 1884, reported that a lightning bolt from a summer storm struck the light station and burned two holes in the bottom of the tower at the base of the stairs. Fortunately, no one was hurt, and no fire was ignited.[4]

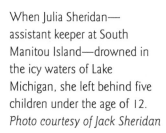

When Julia Sheridan—
assistant keeper at South
Manitou Island—drowned in
the icy waters of Lake
Michigan, she left behind five
children under the age of 12.
Photo courtesy of Jack Sheridan

The possibility of fire was a constant concern at light stations where oil was used to fuel the lamps. One conflagration, though, occurred when a poorly built chimney ignited the keeper's cottage at Pointe aux Barques and drove keeper Catherine Shook and her family out into the elements.[5] They lived in a makeshift lean-to for a time, until a new dwelling could be built.

A lean-to would have provided scant protection from the wolves that roamed the Thumb area at that time. Even bigger predators— black bears—were known to menace the light station at Point Iroquois on Whitefish Bay. One bear dragged a small girl into the woods and devoured her, according to an essay written for the Center for Upper Peninsula Studies.[6]

Physical danger was present even inside the lighthouse itself. While in the Port Sanilac tower on June 13, 1924, Grace Holmes took a tumble through what she called a "trap door" in the lighthouse. Her third-person description of the situation was brief and to the point: "Was on couch four weeks on her back. Broke and fractured ribs and hurt internally. Not all right yet on July 24."[7]

Still another challenge for keepers was keeping a constant supply

The last keeper at Port Sanilac, Grace Holmes—shown here with her keeper husband William—once fell through a trap door at the top of the lighthouse and was out of commission for months. *Photo courtesy of the Schlichting Family Collection*

of healthy, flavorful food on hand. Mainland keepers could hunt near their towers, plant a garden, and even maintain livestock. And they were closer to communities where groceries could be obtained. Island keepers, on the other hand, were more limited in their ability to put food on the table. The fishing was good, to be sure, but they had to rely heavily on stockpiled goods to fill their larders. Interviews with these keepers' children often mention the lack of fresh milk, fruit, vegetables, and eggs in their diets. On periodic trips to the mainland, "we would go to the A&P; they sold [canned] evaporated milk," noted Richard Campbell, son of keeper John Campbell and his wife, Edna. "We would buy cases and cases of it."[8]

Running a close second to food worries was the challenge of finding fresh water to use for drinking, cooking, and bathing. Again, island lights were more problematic in this regard. If there wasn't enough topsoil to dig a privy pit, an outhouse had to be built out over the lake or river—fouling the water supply in the immediate area. One solution was to draw water from the other side of the island. Another was to rig up a rooftop collection system that funneled rainwater down to a cistern. But the system had its flaws. Not only was the water supply governed by the weather, but impurities like bird droppings, particles of roofing material, and dirt could be carried into the tanks. Valves and distilling devices eventually solved the foul water problem.[9]

One would think that, with the many hardships they faced, the health of a light station's inhabitants would be compromised. In fact, lighthouse keepers as a group lived long lives and generally managed to avoid serious injury or illness. After natural causes, the biggest liability was the body of water that their lighthouses illuminated. Many keepers or family members drowned, including keepers Hugh Corgan (brother-in-law of Mary Corgan), Peter Shook (husband of Catherine Shook), Clement Van Riper (husband of Elizabeth Van Riper), and William Wheatley (husband of Mary Ann Wheatley). The keeping couple of Julia and Aaron Sheridan and their young son Robert also met their demise this way.

CHAPTER SEVEN

Were Any Female Keepers Also Mothers?

Many female lighthouse keepers performed their professional duties while raising children, and some had very large families. Among Michigan's most notable keepers who were also mothers are Catherine Shook with eight children and Katherine Marvin with ten.

Keeper's daughter Anna Bowen (later Hoge), standing, and Larry Lane, petting the dog, shared a hair-raising moment on Lake Superior's Passage Island. *Photo courtesy of Crane Hill Publishers/From the book* Lighthouse Families

✳ Keeper's Kids Made Mischief on Passage Island ✳

Left with too much time on their hands, so-called beacon brats could get into a heap of trouble. Anna Bowen Hoge, who grew up at Lake Superior's Passage Island light station, recalled the time she and her sister convinced a young visitor to help them snag a seagull's nest off the side of a cliff:

> [We] tied a rope around unsuspecting Larry and proceeded to lower him over the towering cliff. But we had one problem...we weren't strong enough to pull him back up [and] he wouldn't let go of [the nest] to help himself back up away from the long drop into Lake Superior. I watched as Larry's head sank below the cliff's horizon, then his shirt disappeared, then his upper leg, and finally his sneakers once again faded over the cliff's edge. My sister let go of me and Larry slipped farther toward the sharp rocks below. "I've got you—don't worry!" I yelled to Larry, all the time sounding much more assured than I really was. Meanwhile, my sister ran for help.

As the boy dangled high above the water, Anna's father and the boy's uncle came running—but even they couldn't pull poor Larry to safety. The uncle then launched a rowboat to try to save his nephew from below. Working together, the two men lowered Larry to safety, still hanging on to his prize: the seagull's nest. "Well, my sister and I got spanked," Anna remembered, "and Larry got shipped back to his parents on the next boat to the mainland. That was the last time we saw Larry."[1]

A common challenge for *all* keepers was the education of their children. If their lighthouses were located on the mainland or near a city, the children could be educated in a traditional school setting. Dorotha Story Dodge, whose father kept a light on the Detroit River from 1899 to 1911, remembered how she was transported to class each day: "It was a mile over from [Mamajuda Island] to Wyandotte, and Daddy would row [me] there. And then I walked up to Garfield School."[2] In less populated areas, and especially on islands, keepers took it upon themselves to teach their families "reading, writing, and 'rithmetic," as well as religion.[3]

Starting in 1876, the Lighthouse Service aided keepers in this activity by lending them small, portable collections of reading materials. These traveling libraries included histories such as *The Battle of Mobile Bay*, scientific works such as *Newcomb's Astronomy*, and fiction like *The Five Little Peppers and How They Grew*. Magazines and a copy of the Bible rounded out the collections, which were rotated from light station to light station by inspectors every three months.[4]

To break the monotony of maintaining the light day in and day out, a keeper and her family could engage in a number of pastimes. A common interest keepers' families shared was music: either making it or listening to it on gramophones and, later, the radio. Playing cards and board games or engaging in hobbies helped to while away the time after the station's many chores were done.[5]

If the keeper could find an appropriate replacement, she and her children could also leave the light station for daytrips and visits to friends and family.

CHAPTER EIGHT

Were Female Keepers Treated Differently from Male Keepers?

It was definitely a man's world in the Lighthouse Service of the nineteenth century. For instance, while men could serve at any light station, women were more restricted in their movements—for their own safety. An 1879 circular from Naval Secretary George Dewey to all lighthouse inspectors spelled this out when it noted that:

Though unappreciated during her tenure, Julia Brawn Way is now celebrated at the Bay County Historical Museum in Michigan and the Maine Lighthouse Museum in her home state. *Photo courtesy of the Bay County Historical Society*

Long after Mary Garraty concluded her keeping career at New Presque Isle, she was remembered for her "gentle attentions and kindly hospitality" by the sailing community. *Photo courtesy of the Archives of Michigan*

at isolated stations where there are two or more keepers, no women or children will be allowed to reside, unless by special permission of the Light-House Board. No women will be permitted to reside on a light-ship [a lighthouse on a boat] under any circumstances.[1]

A woman could also be replaced by a man with little or no cause. Both Mary Garraty at New Presque Isle light and Julia Brawn Way at the Saginaw River lights experienced this indignity; their assistant keeper positions were abolished on the same day in 1882 by the Lighthouse Service, only to be reestablished later and filled with men.

Another limitation to women in the service was that, generally, they were not allowed to manage male assistants.[2] Jane Enos, who kept the St. Joseph light, was a rare exception to this rule; she supervised two men during her career. Anna Garraty at Presque Isle Harbor Range lights also supervised one.

Beginning in 1884, all male lighthouse keepers of the U.S. Lighthouse Service were required to wear a regulation uniform that included a double-breasted jacket, vest, and pants of dark blue cloth and a Navy-style cap with a chin strap.[3] Female keepers were given no such uniform, perhaps reflecting the service's lukewarm endorsement of its employees on the distaff side.

Though no particular dress was required of service women, fashions from 1870 to 1910 (the period during which most Michigan women served) dictated that they wear floor-length skirts or dresses

---

✳ Poncher Served, but Did She Ever Get Paid? ✳

An 1874 invoice from the local superintendent of lights requested payment for Mrs. Priscilla Poncher for her work keeping the Grand Traverse light from September 11 to September 30, 1873, at a per diem rate computed on $540 a year.[4] It is thought that Poncher helped keeper Henry Shetterly maintain the light in his final days. (He died on October 21 of that year.) Unfortunately, she was never listed in the annals of the service as an official employee, nor is it known if she was ever compensated for her assistance.

---

and high-heeled footwear—an uncomfortable and unsafe manner of dress for someone required to climb steps, tote oil containers, light lamps, and repair machinery.

Like their male counterparts, women were expected to handle all the heavy work of a light station. But there was one thing on the duty list they were not allowed to do: paint the lighthouse tower.[5] Such a task required the painter to sit high above the ground in a bosun's chair, putting a female light keeper in a distinctly unladylike position.

On the positive side, women were frequently paid the same wages as men, though neither gender got rich from lighthouse-keeping positions.

CHAPTER NINE

What Were the Contributions of Wives of Male Keepers?

In addition to the fifty-plus Michigan women who were official employees of the Lighthouse Service, countless other women served capably alongside their keeper husbands in an unofficial capacity—with no title or salary.

A keeper's wife's primary responsibility was maintaining their residence to the same exacting standards as those of the lighthouse itself. The service's inspectors visited each light station on a quarterly basis to review the performance of the keeper as well as the condition of the station's equipment and the cleanliness of all its buildings.[1] "They'd go right straight through your house, open closet doors and everything," explained Loretta Bush Pearson, who grew up at the White River light. "If things weren't in order, you got a demerit mark for it."[2] Even an unwashed frying pan hidden in an oven could be grounds for being written up.

Not wanting their husbands to be reprimanded, keepers' wives quickly learned to keep everything shipshape. And some were given specific duties to perform. For example, Anna Carlson—wife of Whitefish Point keeper Robert Carlson—functioned as that light station's weather observer, for which she received $10 a month from the Lighthouse Service.[3]

Conscious of the physical strain their husbands endured, wives were also known to take over a shift of light keeping now and again. "A lot of women used to stand watch for the men, if they happened to be working extra hard or...needed a little extra rest," remembered

Captured in a lighthearted moment of dress up on Grassy Island, Edna Campbell was a strong and steady helpmate to her keeper-husband John. *Photo courtesy of Richard Campbell*

James Goudreau, whose father worked at the South Fox Island and Poverty Island lights.[4]

If sickness or absence prevented the male keepers from performing their duties, women assumed complete control of the station. Loretta Bush Pearson recalled a ten-day period when her mother kept the light to enable her father to recover from a blood clot in his leg.[5] And when Mission Point keeper John Lane became incapacitated, he turned over all his responsibilities but the paperwork to his wife, Sarah—for quite a long time. A newspaper article about the couple published in a 1905 edition of the *Grand Rapids Evening Press* noted that she had already served eight unpaid years in his position. Describing her as "well advanced in years," the newspaper nonetheless complimented Sarah on her strong work ethic, saying that the num-

---

✴ Corgan Wives Support Their Keeper Husbands ✴

In Michigan lighthouse history, the name "Corgan" is well known. At least three generations of Corgan men met the challenges of light keeping, and their accomplishments have been recorded for posterity in such volumes as the *Memorial Record of the Northern Peninsula of Michigan*.[6] But behind those men stood two generations of Corgan women whose history is rarely told. Mary Mooney (wife of Charles) was the matriarch of the Corgan clan, accompanying her husband to light keeping assignments at Copper Harbor and Manitou Island. Over the years, she also birthed ten children, three of whom became lighthouse keepers:

- Son James married Mary Raher, and the couple served as a husband-and-wife team at two Lake Superior lighthouses. (James Corgan's wife—featured among the "Sixteen Who Served" in chapter 11—also bore a child named Hugh, who briefly pursued a career in keeping at Manitou Island and Fourteen Mile Point.)
- Son Henry married Catherine Dunn, a steady helpmate to her keeper husband for thirty-one years at Copper Harbor.
- Son Hugh assisted his father at Manitou Island until his untimely death by drowning in 1866.

One of Mary and Charles Corgan's daughters, Elizabeth, chose to marry lighthouse keeper John Power, who served at Copper Harbor from 1869 to 1873.[7]

---

ber of hours she worked "would appall a union man." It went on to describe how, on one stormy evening, the heavy door of the tower blew shut, catching her hand. "So intent was she on the discharge of her duties that she did not realize for several minutes that the end of her finger had been cut off as cleanly as though done with a knife. It never occurred to her that it would be the proper thing to faint away, and she finished her work before she left the tower."[8]

After tending the light all night, Sarah Lane also served as hostess to summertime sightseers to the point. At one time, special days were set aside on which the lighthouse would be open for tours. But, this Lady of the Light was quoted as saying, "So many people were disappointed after taking the long drive [up Old Mission Peninsula], that I really could not refuse to let them in."[9]

John Lane passed away the year after that article appeared, after which the Lighthouse Service finally conferred upon Sarah the official title of keeper.

Perhaps adhering to the axiom that "many hands make light work," several keepers' wives presented their husbands with large families who could share the workload of the light station. The prizewinner must have been the wife of John Malone. In 1875, Malone was appointed keeper of the newly built Menagerie Island light near Isle Royale. Grateful for the appointment, Malone named his first child after the inspector who had given him the job. The Malones continued the tradition of naming their children in honor of the sitting district inspector with the succeeding eleven children, a feat that proved difficult during the year when two inspectors held the post. Julia Malone solved the problem by giving birth to twins.[10]

Under some circumstances, children were called upon to be unofficial keepers. Starting in 1859, at ages 18 and 13 respectively, Effie and Mary McKinley—daughters of Beaver Island Harbor keeper Peter McKinley—ran that light for almost nine years due to their father's poor health.[11] And, in January 1838, while Bois Blanc Island keeper Eber Ward was away from his post, his daughter Emily faced a most daunting task: to save what she could from the lighthouse tower, which was in imminent danger of crashing to the ground in a fearsome storm. From the book *Grandmother's Stories* comes this account:

> Whoever has stood on a perilous height, and seen the mad waters leap and roar and dash with all their might force against the frail structure that supported him can imagine the wild exaltation of soul that filled me through and through to the exclusion of all fear.... . I had but little time, however, to indulge myself in these thoughts, for every wave made the whole tower reel. It took all my strength to carry those great lamps and reflectors down the winding stairs; and sometimes when I would stop to take a breath, and would hear the beat of the waters and

Maebelle L. Mason (signature)

Maebelle Mason—daughter of Mamajuda light keeper Orlo Mason—
proudly sported the lifesaving medals she earned on the Detroit River. *Photo
courtesy of the Bentley Historical Library, University of Michigan/From the
book* History of the Great Lakes, Volume II

feel the shock it gave the tower, it would give me a momentary spasm of terror, but it would be but momentary, for my work must be done, and I had no time for fear. I think I climbed those stairs five times before I got everything movable down.

After gathering her adopted brother and running for the nearby woods, Emily watched the tower collapse into a pile of masonry. "We could see that the house had not been injured, so with thankful hearts we went back and Bolivar was soon in bed and asleep. But I could not sleep for thinking of the ships that were in peril...and tears that I could not restrain wet my pillow that night and succeeding nights."[12]

After the storm subsided, Eber Ward returned safely to the island and his family. The lighthouse was rebuilt later that year.

Maebelle Mason is another example of how keepers' children could be pressed into service if the need arose. In May 1890, a man capsized his rowboat near the Mamajuda light in the Detroit River. Its keeper, Orlo Mason, was away, but his 14-year-old daughter Maebelle launched a punt from the station and rowed more than a mile and back to rescue the man from drowning. For her efforts, Maebelle received lifesaving medals from both the federal government and the Ship Masters Association. "From that day all steamers carrying the

---

❋ Beamer Doesn't Distinguish Herself at Big Bay Point ❋

In terms of hard-working keepers' wives, Jennie Beamer may have been the exception to the rule. Moving to Big Bay Point lighthouse with her husband, George, in 1898, she took his place as an assistant for four months while he was off fighting in the Spanish–American War. Her work ethic during this period and after George returned appears not to have impressed the principal keeper, William Prior. Prior's logbook entry for October 27 reads, "Asst. Beamer complains of being sick and talks of leaving the station to go home to Detroit. He is too high strung for a light keeper's asst.; between himself and his wife this season I imagine that I am keeping a home for the helpless poor instead of a U.S. lighthouse. I and my family having to do the greater part of the work while they receive the pay."[13]

One of the lighthouses on the Detroit River took its name from a woman. Mamajuda was an Indian woman known to camp on the island at the height of fishing season. *Photo courtesy of the Bacon Memorial District Library*

pennant of the association saluted while passing the lighthouse until the young heroine was wedded June 21, 1892," noted John Mansfield in the *History of the Great Lakes, Volume II*.[14]

Perhaps the most unheralded of the "unofficial keepers" was a woman named Henrietta Bergh. The wife of a commercial fisherman on Lake Superior's Bete Grise Bay, she routinely placed a kerosene lantern in an upper window of her house whenever her husband was late coming in off the lake. It wasn't long before other fishermen and ship captains sailing along the eastern shoreline of the Keweenaw Peninsula asked if she would keep a light lit for them, too.

Henrietta then took it upon herself to keep a light burning in her window every evening from dusk until dawn. Her husband made her a large wick lantern with an oil reservoir that would last through the night, and—for many years—she maintained this light with no compensation from the government. Her reward came from those who stopped to thank her or waved as they sailed by.

It is believed that her actions partly prompted the Lighthouse Service to construct the Mendota light at this location in 1895.[15]

CHAPTER TEN

How Long Did Female Keepers Serve?

The 1870s marked the high point of employment of women in Michigan lighthouses, with numbers declining sharply after 1898. In the twentieth century, only thirteen women served the maritime community; of those, nine appeared to be "placeholders" who stayed only a matter of months after a husband's death until a male replacement could be found.

What was the reason for the decline in the number of female keepers, both in the state and nationwide? Officials pointed to changes in technology. A 1948 *Coast Guard Bulletin* noted, "It was the development of steam for [fog] signals and their coal-fired boilers, and the later introduction of heavy duty internal combustion engines [to

---

✺ Colfax Beats Williams's Service Record by Two Years ✺

Though Elizabeth Van Riper Williams's forty-one-year tenure with the Lighthouse Service was impressive, it was not the longest on the Great Lakes. That distinction belongs to Harriet Colfax, who kept the Michigan City, Indiana, light for forty-three years (1861–1904).[1] Nationally, Maria Youghans beat them both with a lighthouse-keeping career that spanned fifty-one years (1867–1918) at the Biloxi lighthouse in Mississippi.[2] Unofficially, Catherine Moore spent fifty-four years (1817–71) at Black Rock Harbor light in Connecticut performing the duties of her ailing father, followed by another seven years on the books of the Lighthouse Service.[3]

Anna Carlson learned her trade
by observing her keeper
husband Robert at four
postings across Wisconsin and
Michigan. *Photo courtesy of the
Great Lakes Shipwreck
Historical Society*

power the signals], which first placed the duties of keepers of lighthouses beyond the capacity of most women."[4] Later advances in the
electrification of lighthouse lamps, including automatic timers and a
device that could replace burned-out bulbs, as well as the introduction of radio beacons and radar, signaled the beginning of the end for
lighthouse keepers of both genders.[5]

As a result, only three Michigan women are listed in Lighthouse
Service records from 1920 on: one of them—Anna Garraty—bridged
the period before, during, and after the first world war. Grace Holmes
served for two years following the death of her husband in 1926. And
the last Michigan woman to serve as a keeper—Frances Wuori Johnson—started her position during World War II and left in 1954. (In-
terestingly, the last male keeper in Michigan wasn't removed from his
post—at Point Betsie—until 1983.)

On the subject of longevity, the average female assistant or principal keeper in Michigan served for about five and a half years. (If you take out of the equation all the women who served for a year or less as they awaited their deceased husbands' replacements, the average term improves to about seven and a half years.) Nine women devoted ten or more years of their lives to the profession, and one—Elizabeth Van Riper Williams—charted forty-one years. The shortest term on record was served by Anna Carlson, wife of a keeper then serving at Marquette Harbor. In 1903, she helped out on Granite Island for nine days until a full-time replacement for a drowned assistant could be found.

CHAPTER ELEVEN

Sixteen Who Served

More than fifty women served at Michigan lighthouses as assistant keepers or keepers starting in 1849 and ending in 1954. While all were dedicated to their jobs, sixteen served with particular distinction. Here are their stories, in order of their first year of official service. (The years that many of these women unofficially served are not included in the dates provided.)

Michigan's First Female Keeper

Catherine Shook
Born 1810, died 1860
Served 1849–51
Pointe aux Barques Lighthouse, Lake Huron

The first female keeper in Michigan served with distinction in the face of great personal tragedy. A New Yorker by birth, Catherine (sometimes spelled Catharine) Doyle Shook moved with her husband, Peter Shook, to Michigan just eleven years after statehood.[1] Peter became keeper of the light located at the critical turning point from Lake Huron into Saginaw Bay. While he labored at the lamp, Catherine had her hands full raising their eight children.

In March 1849, Catherine became ill, and her husband summoned a doctor who sailed to the lighthouse with two lumbermen he employed. After the doctor treated Catherine, Peter and the three men left for Port Huron to acquire supplies. Somewhere north of Lexington, a storm arose and capsized their boat. All four men perished in the accident.[2]

Catherine was appointed keeper in Peter's stead in May 1849, an action that probably saved her and her children from starvation in the sparsely populated area of Michigan's Thumb. Less than a month later, though, another tragedy befell the Shook family: The keeper's house went up in flames.

When the lighthouse inspector arrived, he found Catherine and her children huddled in a small shanty they'd erected. Catherine was suffering from burns she'd sustained while trying to put out the fire. She also suffered the indignity of not being permitted to sign for materials to rebuild the house; her teenage son signed the forms instead.[3]

Fortunately, Catherine was held blameless for the blaze; the inspector theorized that a poorly built chimney was the cause.[4] Her dedication to the light was recognized by the Lighthouse Service, and she continued as its keeper until her voluntary resignation in 1851.

A Keeper in Wartime

Anastasia Truckey
Born 1824, died 1888
Served 1862–65
Marquette Harbor Lighthouse, Lake Superior

For some women, lighthouse keeping wasn't a job; it was their patriotic duty. Such was the case with Anastasia "Eliza" Mercure, born in 1824 in Acadia (now part of Maine).[5] Eliza married Nelson Truckey in 1843; in 1861, he was named lighthouse keeper at Michigan's Marquette Harbor.[6]

The Truckeys raised four children at the lighthouse—a pleasant posting located at the edge of the village. But, in 1862, the drumbeat of the Civil War intruded upon their life; it was then Nelson left to fight with the Michigan Volunteers. His unit saw heavy action at

Vicksburg, the Wilderness, Spotsylvania, the Crater, Petersburg, Cold Harbor, and Appomattox Court House. He didn't return to Michigan until 1865.[7]

In his absence, Eliza was called upon to maintain the light, helping to ensure safe passage for ships carrying ore from the Marquette iron range to northern factories forging firearms, iron cladding for warships, and railroad ties. Historian Frederick Stonehouse considers Eliza's contribution to the war effort critical, suggesting that she may have been "the most important female keeper in the Great Lakes if not the entire country! While Nelson was keeping faith with the Union, Eliza was keeping faith with the mariners."[8]

The Keeper Who Died on Duty

Mary Terry
Born 1816, died 1886
Served 1868–86
Sand Point (Escanaba) Lighthouse, Lake Michigan

One of Michigan's female keepers died under unusual circumstances, and speculation persists to this day about the nature of her death.

A native of Dartmouth, Massachusetts, Mary Thurston married John Terry in 1845. The couple came to Michigan's Upper Peninsula in 1863, when John accepted work as a surveyor with the Chicago & North Western Railway company.[9]

In 1867, he was appointed keeper of a new lighthouse being built at Sand Point on Little Bay de Noc. But, before construction could be completed, he died of tuberculosis. Mary took his place over the objections of local government officials, who strongly opposed the hiring of a woman.[10]

Mary quickly proved herself up to the task. As the local paper, the *Escanaba Iron Port*, reported, she was a "methodical woman, very careful in the discharge of her duties and very particular in the care of the property under her charge."[11] She was even profiled in the *History of the Upper Peninsula of Michigan* (1883)—the only woman featured for Delta County. A careful money manager, she acquired substantial savings and owned land in the city.[12]

Some theorize that her wealth may have led to her death during an early morning fire at the wooden lighthouse in March 1886. Only fragments of her body were found the next day. The south door to the building was discovered standing open—as if it had been forced, not unlocked.[13]

Was the fire set to cover up a crime of robbery or worse? A coroner's jury could find no conclusive evidence and so declared the cause of her death unknown.[14]

A Keeper's Ultimate Sacrifice

Julia Sheridan
Born 1844, died 1878
Served 1872–78
South Manitou Island Lighthouse, Lake Michigan

Though many women made compromises to live the life of a light keeper, Julia Sheridan sacrificed everything in one of the saddest stories in Michigan's lighthouse history.

Julia Moore was a native of New York State and married Aaron Sheridan, a disabled Civil War veteran whom she met in 1865 while he recovered from his wounds. Aaron had no previous lighthouse experience, but—with a determined character and a courageous war record—he secured an appointment as keeper to the South Manitou Island light in 1866. During his tenure, Aaron oversaw the construction of a new light and a steam-powered fog signal.[15]

With the additional responsibilities at the light station, the decision was made to add a first assistant to the roster. Julia, the natural choice for the position, was appointed in 1872.

During their marriage, Julia bore six sons—the last of them born in May 1877.[16] In March of the following year, Aaron, Julia, and their infant Robert made a trip to the mainland with a friend in a small boat. On their return voyage, the boat capsized in the Manitou Passage with tragic results. The *Traverse City Eagle-Herald* recounted the details that followed:

> The wind was blowing quite a gale at the time and it was with great difficulty that a hold could be kept upon the boat.... Twice was Mrs. Sheridan and child assisted upon the boat, which lay bottom side up, but owing to the high sea and the coldness of the water she was unable to retain her grasp upon the rolling treacherous boat and finally sank beneath the waves; while her husband in a last vain attempt to save [them], followed [them] to a watery grave.[17]

The friend hung on to the watercraft for dear life and was ultimately rescued.

Island residents later reported seeing the Sheridans' surviving sons walking along the shore crying for days afterward, looking for their deceased family members. Their bodies were never recovered.[18]

Despite the trauma he experienced at an early age, one of the Sheridan boys—George—grew up to be a lighthouse keeper himself.[19]

Mother to a Lighthouse Dynasty

Mary Garraty
Born 1832, died 1912
Served 1872–82
New Presque Isle Lighthouse, Lake Huron

Born in County Mayo, Ireland, Mary Chambers came to America as a teenager and settled first on Mackinac Island. It was there she met Patrick Garraty (also spelled Garrity), whom she married in 1859.[20] Two years later, the couple moved down the coast of Lake Huron, where Patrick became the last lighthouse keeper at Old Presque Isle and the first keeper at nearby New Presque Isle.[21]

Together they also began a dynasty of Great Lakes lighthouse keepers.

Mary Garraty bore seven children in her prime, including four who grew up to be keepers: John, Thomas, Patrick Jr., and Anna. She also ably assisted her husband at the New Presque Isle light for ten years. (The Lighthouse Service abolished her position in 1882, only to reestablish it eighteen months later and fill it with one of her sons.) During her keeping career, she came to know many captains and sailors on Lake Huron, as well as private yachtsmen. On the occasion of her death, the *Alpena Evening News* noted that "thousands had met her when they put in at Presque Isle for shelter from storms. Many a shipwrecked sailor and passenger has known Mrs. [Garraty's] gentle attentions and kindly hospitality."[22]

Mary and Anna Garraty share the distinction of being the only mother–daughter keepers in Michigan maritime history.

Michigan's Longest-Serving Keeper

Elizabeth Van Riper Williams
Born 1842, died 1938
Served 1872–1913
Beaver Island Harbor and Little Traverse Lighthouses, Lake Michigan

The grande dame of Michigan lighthouse keepers, Elizabeth Whitney Van Riper Williams, was born on Mackinac Island in 1842.[23] Her father, seeking work as a carpenter, moved the family from Mackinac to St. Helena Island to Manistique and finally to Beaver Island, where they encountered the charismatic Mormon leader James Jesse Strang.[24]

Elizabeth wrote about Strang in her 1905 memoir, *A Child of the Sea; and Life among the Mormons*. She talked about her family's early, positive reaction to the man who called himself king: "Strang was so friendly and sent many of his people to call on us."[25] Her father even built the Mormon leader a house. But the good feelings about Strang and his followers soon turned to suspicion and later to fear, as some took to harassing Gentiles (their name for nonbelievers) like the Whitneys.

In 1852, tensions reached a head, and the Gentiles were given ten days to join the Mormons or leave the island.[26] The Whitneys chose to depart, first settling in Charlevoix and later making a home in Traverse City, until news reached them that Strang had been assassinated by two disgruntled followers.

Shortly after, Elizabeth's family returned to Beaver Island to pick up the pieces of their life. While there, she resumed a friendship with the McKinley family. Peter McKinley had been named keeper of the Beaver Island Harbor lighthouse in 1859, but his poor health dictated that two of his daughters—Effie and Mary—help him. "The two girls and myself were like sisters as time went on," wrote Elizabeth.[27]

In 1860, Elizabeth married Clement Van Riper, who owned a cooper shop on the island. Within two years, he was appointed a government schoolteacher to American Indians on neighboring Garden Island, and later the couple engaged in a fishing business.

In 1869, Peter McKinley resigned his appointment at the Beaver Island lighthouse, and Van Riper was named to take his place. "My husband having now very poor health, I took charge of the care of the lamps; and the beautiful lens in the tower was my special care. On stormy nights, I watched the light that no accident might happen. We burned the lard oil, which needed great care, especially in cold weather, when the oil would congeal and fail to flow fast enough to the wicks. In long nights, the lamps had to be trimmed twice each night and sometimes oftener."[28]

One terrible evening in 1872, the Van Ripers could hear the flapping of sails and see lights flashing in the distance; a ship was in distress. After a struggle, it reached the harbor and then sank. Elizabeth's husband valiantly tried to assist, but he drowned in the attempt.

Though consumed by grief, she knew what had to be done:

> I was weak from sorrow, but realized that though the life that was dear to me had gone, yet there were others out on the dark and treacherous waters who needed to catch the rays of the shining light from my lighthouse tower. Nothing could rouse me but that thought, then all my life and energy was given to the work which now seemed was given me to do.

Elizabeth and Daniel Williams were a devoted couple. At the conclusion of her long career, they retired to nearby Charlevoix and died within 28 hours of each other. *Photo courtesy of the Harbor Springs Area Historical Society*

She finished the chapter with a bit of verse:

> Let our lamps be brightly burning
> For our brothers out at sea—
> Then their ships are soon returning,
> Oh! how glad our hearts will be.
> There are many that have left us,
> Never more will they return;
> Left our hearts with sorrows aching,
> Still our lamps must brightly burn.[29]

Despite her loss, Elizabeth did manage to find love again, marrying photographer Daniel Williams in 1875.

As many of their friends began to move from the island to the mainland in that decade, Elizabeth and Daniel decided to go ashore, too, motivating Elizabeth to petition the Lighthouse Service for a

Little Traverse lighthouse was the only one to have a woman—Elizabeth Van Riper Williams—as its first keeper. *Photo courtesy of the Archives of Michigan*

transfer. In 1884, she was privileged to light the new Little Traverse lamp for the first time. "We were soon at work putting our house in order, and the beautiful lens in the tower seemed to be appealing to me for care and polishing," she noted.[30]

Over time, Elizabeth grew to love the community and her new lighthouse as much as her first. "On the end of the Point stands the lighthouse with its red light flashing out at night over the waters," she exclaimed in her book, "looking like a great red ruby set with diamonds as the electric lights are shining around the bay and harbor. What more is needed of nature's beauty to make the picture complete?"[31]

In 1913, after forty-one years of service to the sailors of Lake Michigan, she retired to Charlevoix with her husband.[32]

A Keeper against All Odds

> *Julia Brawn Way*
> Born 1816, died 1889
> Served 1873–82
> Saginaw River Lighthouses, Lake Huron

This keeper persisted in performing her duties to the best of her abilities despite frequent changes in her job status.

Julia Toby (sometimes spelled Tobey) was born in Hallowell, Maine, in 1816 and married Peter Brawn when she was twenty-five. As a couple, they moved first to Ontario and later to Michigan. In 1866, he was appointed keeper of the light at the mouth of the Saginaw River.[33]

Lighthouse Service records note that Peter was disabled, requiring considerable assistance from Julia in maintaining the light. After his death in 1873, she was named keeper in her own right, with help from her teenage son, Dewitt. During her tenure, she oversaw the construction of a new brick lighthouse on the site.[34]

In the mid-1870s, Julia married a river pilot named George Way and was demoted to assistant keeper reporting to her husband. Julia's position was then abolished in 1882, effectively ending her career. Seven months later, the Lighthouse Service reestablished the assistant keeper position at the light and filled it with a man.

George passed away in 1883. Julia lived on for six more years until her death at age seventy-three. A newspaper of the time eulogized her as "a lady who possessed noble traits of character. Being ever ready to aid the distressed and care for the needy. As she lived, so she died, a loving wife, a kind mother [of six] and Christian woman."[35]

A Keeper's Adventure

> *Mary Corgan*
> Born 1856, died 1893
> Served 1873–75, 1877–83
> Manitou Island and Gull Rock Lighthouses, Lake Superior

Mary Raher, the daughter of a ship's captain, was born in Ireland in the mid-nineteenth century and settled with her parents in the western Upper Peninsula.[36] She lived a short life, but an active one thanks in part to her marriage to a lighthouse keeper named James Corgan.

Mary met James while he taught school in L'Anse, Michigan. After marrying at sixteen, she served as assistant to her husband at two Michigan lighthouses in the 1870s and 1880s. While working at the Manitou Island light near Lake Superior's Keweenaw Peninsula, James and then-pregnant Mary had the most amazing experience. James described it in his logbook for July 15, 1875, in this way (misspellings have not been corrected):

> Principle keeper started 8:00 p.m. in the station boat with wife for Copper Harbor (distant 14 miles) with anticipation of increase soon after arriving. When one and one half miles east of Horseshoe Harbor, Mrs. Corgan gave birth to a rollicking boy; all things lovely, had everything comfortable aboard. Sea a dead calm."[37]

After the child was delivered, there was no need to seek help in Copper Harbor so the craft was turned about and arrived back at the lighthouse with its new resident. His parents named him James.

Besides young James, who later became the warden at Marquette State Prison, Mary bore seven other children, including a future Baraga County prosecutor and another who entered the Lighthouse Service like his parents. Mary died in 1893 of an undisclosed illness in a Chicago hospital, her youngest child not yet two.[38]

The People's Keeper

Caroline Litogot Antaya
Born 1845, died 1903
Served 1874–85
Mamajuda Lighthouse, Detroit River

The Mamajuda lighthouse that once illuminated the Detroit River at Wyandotte is all but forgotten; the light was removed in 1921 and the

Caroline Litogot (later Antaya) poses with sons Edward at left and Artemus, also known as Arthur. Arthur grew up to become a Michigan keeper himself at Bar Point light on the Detroit River. *Photo courtesy of the Benson Ford Research Center/The Henry Ford*

island it stood upon has been reduced to a sandbar by the fast current.[39] But, from 1874 to 1885, it was home to Caroline Litogot Antaya, and she fought to keep it that way.

Born Caroline Taylor in Livonia Township, Michigan, she married Barney Litogot—an uncle of carmaker Henry Ford—the year the Civil War started. Barney served with honor in the Union army, losing several fingers on his right hand at Gettysburg. He then returned to Michigan and took up the profession of farming.[40] During the postwar period, Caroline gave birth to three boys—two of whom died as infants. In early 1873, Barney was named keeper at the Mamajuda light, and their fourth son was born. By the end of that year, Barney had passed away of tuberculosis.[41]

After Barney died, the superintendent of Detroit lighthouses named Caroline acting keeper, probably out of sympathy for her loss.[42]

Six months later, however, the district lighthouse inspector removed Caroline from her office, citing ill health and incompetence; he then appointed a man to take her place. But the community near the light rose to Caroline's defense, even enlisting the help of Michigan's U.S. Senator Zachariah Chandler to secure her reappointment. "The vessel men all say that she keeps a very excellent light," noted Chandler in his appeal to the secretary of the Light-House Board, "and I think it very hard to remove this woman, who is faithful and efficient, and throw her upon the world with her children entirely destitute. . . ."[43] Within two months, she was reinstated with full duties.

In 1882, she married Adolph Antaya, owner of a large fishery near Port Huron.[44] She maintained her position at the lighthouse, however, and continued keeping until her voluntary resignation three years later.

Caroline and Barney's youngest son Artemus (also called Arthur) followed in his parents' footsteps, serving as an assistant keeper in the early twentieth century at Oswego Breakwater light in New York and at Bar Point on the Detroit River.[45]

The Keeper Who Managed Men

Jane Enos
Born circa 1826, died ?
Served 1876–81
St. Joseph Lighthouse, Lake Michigan

Even among the groundbreaking women who kept lights in Michigan, Jane Enos was exceptional. She was one of the few women known to have supervised male assistants—a feat she repeated twice in her career.

Jane Drew was born in New York state circa 1826. After migrating to Michigan, she married a Berrien County farmer named John Enos, with whom she later had at least eight children.[46]

John was named keeper at the St. Joseph light in 1861 and served the mariners of Lake Michigan for fifteen years until his death in 1876. Upon his passing, Jane was named acting keeper—a title she held for two years while carrying out all of her late husband's responsibilities. During that time, she was permitted to supervise a male assistant keeper named M. B. Ross. For her efforts, she was paid a salary of $600 a year, which was commensurate with male keepers' salaries of the time.[47]

In 1878, the qualifier "acting" was removed from her title. In 1880, her son-in-law William Dudley replaced Ross as her assistant and served under her for the next fifteen months. According to the 1880 federal census, William, his wife (Jane's daughter Julia), and their child lived in the lighthouse with Jane and her youngest son.[48]

In a move viewed as politically motivated, both Jane and William were removed from their offices on the same day in 1881. President James Garfield appointed Curtis Boughton, a Civil War veteran, in her place.[49]

The *St. Joseph Traveler Herald* newspaper reported that no accident or mishap ever befell a ship in St. Joseph due to the failure of the lighthouse during the time that Jane had charge of it.[50]

The Reluctant Keeper

Lucy Gramer
Born 1875, died ?
Served 1898
Ecorse Range Light, Detroit River

Little is known of Lucy Gramer's early years in Michigan as the daughter of German immigrants.[51] But it may be said that when she married August (Gus) Gramer, her life took a decidedly dramatic turn.

Gus, who was born in New York City, signed on to a whaling crew when he was just fifteen, then spent years sailing the seas in the service of the U.S. Navy—even surviving a shipwreck. When he finally settled down, he chose another maritime career: that of light keeping on the Great Lakes.[52] Over the course of his career, he was assigned to the lightship *Limekiln Crossing* and the Ecorse Range light in the Detroit River, the Monroe lighthouse, and the Toledo Harbor light in Ohio.

In 1892, before Gus's lightship experience, Lucy presented him with their first child: a daughter. Three years later, he moved his family into the keeper's cottage at the Ecorse Range light. But his wanderlust soon got the best of him; in 1898, he made the ill-timed choice to leave Lucy in charge of the light in the same month she gave birth to their son, while he went off to fight in the Spanish–American War.[53]

In June 1900, when the federal census was taken in Ecorse Township, the four Gramers were recorded as living in the same household.[54] By August of that year, however, Lucy had grown unhappy with her husband and moved herself and the children out of the lighthouse and in with her father in Detroit. It is unknown what exactly transpired between the couple to prompt their separation. But the die was cast for their divorce when Gus shared the details of their disintegrating marriage with the *Detroit Tribune*. The newspaper reported how Gus

At Ecorse Range light on the Detroit River, two wives of keeper Gus Gramer replaced him while he took temporary leaves. Lucy Gramer served in 1898 and Mary Gramer in 1906. *Photo courtesy of the Bacon Memorial District Library*

called upon his wife the other night and…urged her to come back with the children and live with him, but she demurred, and after acknowledging how good he had been to her, she fell on her knees, Gus says, and between her sobs confessed that she really preferred [a former roomer of the Gramers]…although he is not handsome.

Gramer then claimed to have called his old friend in, made the man kneel beside his wife, and placed Lucy's hand in that of the other person. "Lucy," he is reported to have said, "be good to the children; Charlie, be good to Lucy, as she has been a good wife to me." He told the reporter that he concluded the meeting by taking Lucy and Charlie out to an ice cream parlor.[55]

Unfortunately for Gus, Mrs. Gramer disputed his account, particularly the part about her falling on her knees. She replied:

> If Gus was half as good [as Charlie], it would be better for him, and there would probably have never been any trouble. When he says that I am going to marry another man as soon as I get a divorce, he is drawing on his imagination. There is no truth in it and I never fell down on my knees to Gus and confessed anything. Everybody knows that I am full of the old Nick, but everybody except Gus knows also that it is all honest fun and no meanness and Gus ought to know that too."[56]

Though Gus had agreed to give Lucy custody of their children, she apparently didn't trust him to keep his word. She told the paper that she was going to "keep a sharp lookout" to see that he didn't get any legal advantage when she was not looking.

Gus maintained his keeping position at Ecorse through the divorce proceedings and quickly married again—this time to a woman named Mary. Her name appears as an acting keeper at Ecorse for two weeks in 1906.[57]

The Fertile Keeper

Katherine Marvin
Born 1849, died ?
Served 1898–1904
Squaw Point Lighthouse, Lake Michigan

Many of Michigan's female light keepers were mothers, some of sizable families. But Katherine "Kate" Marvin took the prize in this category, giving birth to ten children before her childbearing years were over.[58]

Born in Detroit in 1849, she married Lemuel (sometimes spelled Lemeul) Marvin when she was just sixteen. A Baptist minister by training, Lemuel also served in the Civil War, where his injuries compromised his health. As compensation for his sacrifice, an influential friend in Washington, DC, obtained a keeper's appointment for him at Squaw Point lighthouse on Little Bay de Noc in the Upper Peninsula—an idyllic if isolated place to raise their brood.[59]

Lemuel held his position for only six months before he died suddenly of pneumonia, leaving Kate with four of their ten children still living at home.[60] To support her remaining family, Kate decided to apply for her late husband's position and was given the job for a probationary period of three months. By March 1898, she had secured the official appointment.[61]

At Squaw Point, Kate was separated from her nearest neighbors by six miles of piney woods, and it was a twenty-minute row across the bay in fair weather to visit the village of Gladstone. Despite these conditions, Kate thrived in her new life and enjoyed the comfortable home the government provided as well as the regular shipments of supplies. "I wouldn't want to work for a better firm than Uncle Sam," she once said.[62]

She served contentedly as Squaw Point's keeper for a term of six years.

A Keepers' Daughter Becomes Keeper

Anna Garraty
Born 1872, died 1937
Served 1903–26
Presque Isle Harbor Range Lighthouses, Lake Huron

Many families of lighthouse keepers were known to have worked the Great Lakes. Anna Garraty (also known as Anne Garrity) was a member of a family that served a collective 184 years.[63]

Anna's father, Patrick, started the tradition when he was appointed keeper at Old Presque Isle lighthouse in 1861. When a second, taller lighthouse was constructed a mile to the north, Patrick and his family moved there. At New Presque Isle, he was assisted by his wife, Mary, for ten years and later by their son Thomas. In 1890, son

Patrick Jr. became assistant and, the following year, Patrick Sr. traded places with Thomas, who'd been keeping the Presque Isle Harbor Range lights. In 1905, brother John was named Thomas's assistant.

In 1903, Patrick Sr. retired from the Lighthouse Service, and daughter Anna—age thirty-one—was appointed in his place at the range lights. She was said to have sat in a rocking chair on her front porch and rocked all night, watching the lights to make sure they stayed lit.[64] She served an impressive twenty-three years as a keeper, and for three years—from 1923 to 1926—she also managed a male assistant: a rare privilege for a woman.

Long before her keeping career began, however, Anna suffered an unspeakable tragedy; she was assaulted by an assistant keeper serving under her father. Patrick Garraty's keeper's log entry for June 19, 1889, describes what happened (misspellings have not been corrected):

> My Assistant [...] is now in the county jail. The Sherrif arrested him with a criminal warrant for the crime of rape on my Daughter Annie and thretened her life and tried to choke her. He obtained a hearing before a Justice and was bound over to the term of Circuit Court which will be in October next.[65]

Following journalistic practice of the day, Anna was named in a newspaper report of the assistant's arraignment. The *Presque Isle County Advance* described her as "a beautiful young lady of about 17 summers [who] comes from a most highly respected family."[66] The assistant was tried for his crime in nearby Rogers City, but the results of that trial are unknown due to a fire that destroyed all news accounts from that period. Lighthouse Service records show, however, that he was removed from his position at New Presque Isle later that year.

A Nurse and a Keeper

Sarah Lane
Born 1840, died circa 1918
Served 1906–7
Mission Point Lighthouse, Lake Michigan

Born Sarah Noyes on October 16, 1840, in Williamstown, Massachusetts, this lighthouse keeper was prepared early in life to accept responsibility when at age four she lost her mother.[67] As a grown woman, she put that experience to work nursing an ailing husband while maintaining a light without title or pay.

Sarah was the wife of John Lane, a steamer captain who sailed a route between Buffalo and Duluth. After his sailing days were done, he took a job as assistant keeper of Michigan's St. Clair Flats South Channel Range lights, which he held for a year until he was transferred to the keeper position at Mission Point light in northwest Lower Michigan.[68] He and Sarah moved to the picturesque wooden lighthouse in 1881.

The Lanes served together—she in an unofficial role—for more than fifteen years before John's health began to fail. Sarah then assumed the principal keeper's duties. Handling all but the paperwork, she devoted her middle years to keeping the light lit at the end of Old Mission Peninsula. "It is a matter of great rejoicing to both Mr. and Mrs. Lane that...there have never been any serious wrecks at the Point," noted the *Grand Rapids Evening Press*.[69]

Sarah was also complimented for the profusion of beautiful flowers that encircled the lighthouse as well as for her demeanor. "Always cheery, never showing her weariness, it is no wonder that Mrs. Lane is the idol of the summer visitors at Old Mission, as well as one of the best loved among the old residents [of the area]," said the newspaper.[70]

John Lane died of pneumonia in 1906, and Sarah was officially appointed in his stead. But her tenure lasted only three months before she retired at the age of sixty-seven. She lived with her daughter Minnie for a time, as well as her grandson Maurice, before passing away.

A Keeper and a Journalist

Grace Holmes
Born 1863, died 1935
Served 1926–28
Port Sanilac Lighthouse, Lake Huron

At Thunder Bay Island, a romance blossomed between a keeper's daughter, Grace Sinclair, and her father's assistant, William Holmes. After the two married and had children, they were posted to this light, at Port Sanilac. *Photo courtesy of the Archives of Michigan*

Grace Holmes was a third-generation lighthouse keeper, with close ties from birth to the water. Her grandfather, John Sinclair Sr., and father, John Sinclair Jr., were sailors on the Great Lakes who later took up the profession of keeping.[71] Grace met and married William Holmes—a member of the U.S. Lifesaving Service—while living with her parents at the Thunder Bay Island light. The Sinclairs encouraged William to join the Lighthouse Service instead.[72] His first assignment was assisting her father in Thunder Bay, thirteen miles from the harbor at Alpena.

As the Holmes's children reached school age, the couple looked for ways to educate them so far from the mainland. Grace's uncle Richard Morris—at the time a lighthouse keeper in Michigan's

Thumb—came up with the solution, offering William his assignment in Port Sanilac so the Holmes family could live at a posting close to a school.[73]

William Holmes became principal keeper at Port Sanilac in 1893 and enjoyed good health until a bout of rheumatism and neuritis in 1922 nearly took his life.[74] Medical problems plagued him in the years thereafter, and he required Grace's help to keep the lamp lit.

In 1926, William died. Given the experience she accumulated during his period of bad health, Grace was easily able to succeed him as keeper and—according to Lighthouse Service records—remained there until the light was fully automated in 1928.

In addition to being the last keeper at Port Sanilac, Grace distinguished herself by keeping a journal from the time her family arrived in the community until her death. Described by local historian Cathi Bulone Campbell as a treasure trove of information, the journal documents the people and the lives they lived during their time in Sanilac Township, Carsonville, Forester, Sandusky, Applegate, and Lexington. "She journaled like a lighthouse keeper," Campbell said, "commenting on the weather and on events in a very matter-of-fact way."[75] An excerpt of Grace's writing is included here:

Jan. 16th, 1911: [Commercial fishermen] Will & Herb Walker were out after their nets and unable to get back on account of drifting ice. A party from here tried to reach them this evening but was forced to return. The life-saving crew at Harbor Beach were telephoned for and started down with teams at 9:30 p.m. Keeper lighted the light for them.

Jan. 17th, 1911: The life-saving crew and boat arrived at 4 a.m. They launched their boat at 5 a.m. and started southeast looking for the Walker boys, was in sight until dark battling with the ice. Keeper lighted up.

Jan. 18th, 1911: The tug "J. M. Diver" from Port Huron arrived at 2 a.m. and again at 9 a.m. They picked up the Walker boys about midnight last night 6 miles south and 4 miles east of this [Port Sanilac] light. They landed them here at 9 a.m. O.K. The lifesavers landed at Lexington at 8 a.m. after being out in the ice 27 hours. They arrived here at 2 p.m.

Jan. 19th, 1911: The life-saving crew left this morning with their boat on a sleigh.[76]

Michigan's Last Female Keeper

Frances Wuori Johnson
Born 1921
Served 1944–54
White River Lighthouse, Lake Michigan

In the 1920s, as technology turned from oil to electricity, the Lighthouse Service began quietly to phase out women from its ranks. But Frances Gilmer didn't get the memo. In fact, she didn't even start her keeping career until 1944.

While vacationing in west Michigan that year, she met and fell in love with Leo Wuori, keeper at the White River light. Within months, they were married and she moved into the picturesque brick structure that marked the waterway between Lake Michigan and White Lake.

As Leo's assistant, she assumed many of the responsibilities of maintaining the electrified light, including winding the weights that revolved the lens twice a night and cleaning its prisms. "Those glass prisms reflected all that light," she explained. "And then, besides that, the two sides of the light that were brass on the outside were sterling silver on the inside. I had to keep those polished up, so they reflected the light also."[77]

While up in the lantern, she could see storms developing from miles away. "We had two big fish boats that went out every day from across the channel," she remembered. "I'd no more get up in the light to check on how a storm was coming, and [I'd] see out on the horizon these two fish boats…steaming like crazy to get into port. They always made it, but boy, they had a tough time. They hauled in tons and tons

Frances Wuori Johnson stumped the panel of television's *What's My Line?* in 1953 when they couldn't guess her unique profession. *Photo courtesy of Frances Marshall*

of whitefish and Lake Michigan salmon and they made a good living, but it was a treacherous living."[78]

On quiet days, Frances took time to perfect her swimming stroke. This talent came in handy, as tourists tended to underestimate Lake Michigan's strong riptides then found themselves drifting farther and farther from the shore. Many were the times that Frances risked her life to save a floundering man, woman, or child: "One [woman had] a really chunky build, and finally I had to just about knock her out and then pull her in because I couldn't do anything with her. And she said, 'You hurt me.' And I said, 'Well, it was either that or let you die.'"[79]

After four years of marriage, Leo and Frances called it quits and both moved away from the lighthouse. But the lure of the lake was strong, prompting her to petition the Lighthouse Service to return to duty. She married a man named Herald Johnson and, in 1949, was welcomed back to White River—this time as a full-fledged keeper.

White River was the posting of the last female lighthouse keeper in Michigan: Frances Wuori Johnson. *Photo courtesy of the Archives of Michigan*

During her second stint at the lighthouse, she was asked to appear on national television. "I took a train from Holland to Port Huron [across Canada to New York State], down the river, and into New York City," Frances explained. "And I was on *What's My Line?* that night." She stumped the celebrity panelists with her unusual (for a woman) profession. For participating in the show, she received a check for $50. Afterward, she was deluged with telegrams and letters from people asking her to "get them a job like I had."[80]

Frances left the lighthouse for good in 1954 and settled into a quieter life as an office administrator in nearby Montague.

While speaking at the 2008 opening of the Michigan Women's Historical Center exhibit on Michigan lady lighthouse keepers, she was asked if she missed her previous life at the light. "You bet," she exclaimed. "I'd go back to it in a minute, if they'd let me."[81]

Emily Fish, an Albion, Michigan, native who kept the Point Piños light on California's Monterey Bay, weathered the 1906 San Francisco earthquake. *Photo courtesy of the Monterey Public Library, California History Room*

✳ Michigan Woman Called California's "Socialite Keeper" ✳

Though she never served in Michigan, Albion's Emily Fish made a name for herself in the Lighthouse Service when she assumed the keeper's position at Point Piños near Monterey, California, in 1893. A widow of means, she filled the keeper's cottage with antiques and fine art and transformed the bare, windswept lawn into a colorful tapestry of trees and flowers. Despite her official duties, which by all accounts she performed admirably, she still found time to entertain Monterey society at lighthouse dinner parties, where French poodles greeted her guests.[82]

CHAPTER TWELVE

An Interview with Frances (Wuori Johnson) Marshall

What follows is an excerpted version of an oral history interview conducted in 2007 with Michigan's last female lighthouse keeper Frances Marshall. She served at the White River light on Lake Michigan. The interviewer is the author.

The full interview is available in audio and print versions in the archives of the Great Lakes Lighthouse Keepers Association.

PM: We're talking with Frances Marshall about her experiences as a female lighthouse keeper. Can you tell me about your life before you came to White River?

FM: I was born in Noble, Georgia, on November 5, 1921. When I was quite small, we moved to Michigan and I grew up in Pontiac. I graduated from Pontiac High School. I never did like Pontiac. My dad had a grocery store there which I worked at fourteen hours a day. So I decided to get a job in industry where I could have some vacation time. When I got a week's vacation, I decided to spend it on Lake Michigan. I wrote to chambers of commerce all up and down this part of Lake Michigan to find out what they had. Of course, I got all kinds of mail, and I chose Sylvan Beach Guest House right down the beach from the [White River] lighthouse. I didn't even see the lighthouse then, but Sylvan Beach seemed like a pretty reasonable place to stay so I decided to stay a week there. I was down on the beach soaking up some sun and this dog came along. Of course, I love dogs, I love any animal. I petted him and he liked that, so he stayed around and I petted him some more. And we made good friends. When I left, he followed me and I kept telling him he had to go home. He finally wandered off to the lighthouse, but I didn't know where he was going…

The following year, I got a week's vacation again, and so I went back to the Sylvan Beach hotel. I met Timmy again, the dog. So I decided I'd follow him home. I said, "Let's go home, Timmy," and he took off but he always looked back to see if I was coming. He led me to the lighthouse. Then I met Leo [Wuori].

PM: He was the keeper at that time?

FM: Yes. They had just completed redoing the whole lighthouse inside.

PM: What year would this have been?

FM: [Around 1944] because they had closed up the Coast Guard station across the channel, and they had a furnace out of there that they put in the lighthouse. It had never had a furnace before. Just had a space heater. Then they put a refrigerator and a nice big sink and countertop in, really fixed it up. Sealed up the hole where the old stove used to sit and plastered that over and painted it. Oh, they painted the whole upstairs and downstairs. It was really a quite comfortable house when I moved into it, because it had a furnace and it always had running water, but it had a water heater and was really quite up to date.

Well, anyway, Leo and I met through Timmy. [Laugh.] So I spent the rest of the week visiting back and forth at the lighthouse. Then we wrote back and forth when I got home. And he came down to Pontiac to see me. Then I went up to Champion, Michigan, to see his folks. We decided to get married in August.

PM: That same year?

FM: August of [1944].

PM: That same summer?

FM: Yeah. Then he decided the next spring that his time was up in the Coast Guard, [that he wanted to] muster out.

I had told him when we discussed marriage, "Just keep it in the back of your mind: I will never, never live in the Upper Peninsula." So then when he decided to muster out, he said, "And then we can go to the Upper Peninsula." And I said, "Not me!" So he went one way and I went the other. [Laugh.]

PM: Then you came back as keeper the following year in 1949 and resigned in 1954. Does that sound about right?

FM: I went back to Pontiac and that's when I met [my daughter] Holly's father. And we got married and moved back to the lighthouse.

PM: What year did you get married?

FM: I think we got married in 1950. Because Leo had been gone a couple of years by then.

PM: Let's go backwards for a minute. You were Leo's assistant [at lighthouse keeping] when you were married? You assisted him?

FM: Assisted him? He didn't do anything. He liked to fish and hunt and stuff like that. That's what he did. He found out that he could do that and I could do all the work. So I, of course, fixed the meals and did the dishes and waxed the floors. The floors were all wooden floors, hardwood. I had to scrub them, and then wax them with paste wax, and then polish that. Gads! And then I had to keep the light clean every day.

PM: Was the light electrified when you got there?

FM: It had an electric bulb, but [the light] had weights on it like a cuckoo clock that turned it around. We had to wind the weights twice a night.

PM: So you just set the alarm clock and got up to wind the weights.

FM: Before I moved back into the light—I was gone about a year, I guess—they had electrified the light completely. It had an electric motor on it that turned it on earlier in the winter and later in the summer, and turned it off the opposite way. But you still had to clean the light and polish the brass on it and keep it going. And, of course, that was the reason I got the job, because I had such good experience at the light.

PM: Who did it between when you left and came back? No-body?

FM: Yes, there was a couple there. Jeepers, they made me so mad; they robbed everything they could put their hands on at the lighthouse. Some of it I never got back. I had some great big maps of the lighthouse and where the water line was on certain dates in those years, way back. They took all that stuff with them or burned it or something. People are so dumb.

76

PM: That is a shame.

FM: Yes, it is.

PM: Was there any difficulty in getting the appointment either as assistant or as keeper because you were a woman, or was that not a problem?

FM: No, it was never a problem. When I married Leo, I didn't know I was going to be doing all the work. But I did and let it go at that. Then when I found out it was going to be available for ordinary people, I called Cleveland and he said, "Well, come on down and we'll have a chat." So I did. He said, "We've had some bids on the job, but they're not near as good as [your credentials]. So you get the job."

PM: Was he the inspector? Who was Cleveland?

FM: He was a Coast Guard officer. He used to come up, used to be our inspector. I told him, if the light ever came available for regular civilians, to give me a call. And I gave him my mother's number. He remembered and he called me.

PM: How much were you paid?

FM: $30 a month. [Laugh.]

PM: And you lived there year-round.

FM: Oh, yes.

PM: What did you like best about the work? What were some of the more enjoyable aspects?

FM: When I went up to clean the light, I could always have a new view of the area; it was always changing. I got to see a lot of stuff from up there [such as] storms coming in over Lake Michigan. That was always interesting! I'd read the weather forecasts all the time.

We had two big fish boats that went out every day from across the channel. I'd no more get up in the light to check on how a storm was coming, and I could see out on the horizon these two fish boats steaming like crazy to get into port. [Laugh.] They always made it, but boy they had a tough time. They hauled in tons and tons of whitefish and Lake Michigan salmon and they made a good living, but it was a treacherous living.

PM: Is that what most of the ship traffic was coming this way?

FM: Yes. And the Coast Guard boat would come in once in the spring to check the buoys and stuff like that.

PM: How often did the Coast Guard supply you with what you needed for the lighthouse?

FM: They didn't supply me with anything. [Laugh.] All they supplied me with was a dog to fight my dog.

PM: They gave you a dog?

FM: No, they had a dog on board, then they let down the gangplank. The minute they let down the gangplank, here came this dog. Timmy thought he owned the whole lighthouse, the yard, and everything else. Oh, that made him so mad. Of course, he took off after the dog. Then a fight would start. I'd say, "You'll have to separate them. I can't separate them; they're too big." And the captain would separate them and take his dog back and put him on the boat.

PM: What kind of dog was Timmy?

FM: Timmy was a mixture of a bulldog and a terrier. He had a nose like a terrier. And he had the short legs like a bull. His whole body was like a bull. He was big and heavy, but he had short, fat legs and couldn't run very fast. But he sure was a nice dog. And he thought everything of me.

PM: Did you get to keep him when you separated from Leo?

FM: No, I didn't get to keep him.

PM: That's too bad. What didn't you like about lighthouse keeping? What were the bad parts?

FM: Scrubbing floors, I guess.

PM: I heard that you had to fish people out of the lake.

FM: Oh, yes. The channel wasn't as wide as it is now. People would take their kids out by that channel. The adults would be in front with the kids running behind them to catch up. Well, then, all of a sudden, you'd hear SPLASH and the kids were in the water. So then they'd start hollering, "Help! Help!" I had to go and pull them out of the channel.

PM: Dive in to get them? Or just throw them a life preserver?

FM: They were such little kids; they wouldn't know what to do with a life preserver. So I dove in the water and pulled them out. They did have sense enough to paddle around until I could get a hold of them. Then I gave their parents a sermon on keeping track of your kids. I don't know whether it did any good or not. [Laugh.]

PM: Were there many shipwrecks in your time?

FM: No. But one time in a huge storm, we found the wreckage of an old sailing ship. Its keel washed up on the channel wall. It was just the keel and some sideboards. We even sent them to Lansing, and they identified [the ship they were attached to].

PM: Did you spend much time sailing in Lake Michigan?

FM: No, I spent most of the time swimming. We did have a friend that had a thirty-eight-foot sailboat. Oh, I loved sail boating; it was nice and quiet not to have that motor running all the time. You could just float along in the water. He'd come up once in a while and take us for a sailboat ride. But mostly I swam.

PM: Quite a lot?

FM: Oh yes. I was in the water every day. I was as brown as a bear by the end of the summer.

PM: What did Holly's dad do for a living?

FM: He was an accountant.

PM: And so he was able to do that here.

FM: He worked for Howmet.

PM: But he lived at the lighthouse.

FM: Yes.

PM: He didn't assist you in keeping the lighthouse?

FM: No, nobody wanted that job.

PM: How often did the inspector come by?

FM: Back when I was first at the lighthouse under Cleveland, jeepers he seemed to be there every time I turned around. I think he was there about every other month. When I came back again, it was no longer under the Coast Guard. Well, it was under the Coast Guard, but they weren't so persnickety. They didn't come up and bother me about inspectors at all. They knew I was taking care of the light and doing a good job.

PM: Did they wear white gloves?

FM: That's what they used to do when I first was there. They had white gloves on and they wrote down everything.

PM: Did you ever get written up?

FM: Well, they wrote up everything they didn't like. And then you got so many dismerits of some sort. But it never affected me.

PM: But when you came back as a full keeper, they weren't as concerned about that?

FM: They didn't send an inspector up at all. He [Cleveland] asked me if I thought I could run the light and do everything that needed to be done. And I said, "Well, I did it for so many years and so I think I could do it again." They had no problems with me. [Laugh.]

PM: Was your daughter Holly born at the lighthouse or during that time?

FM: She was born at Shelby Hospital [now Lakeshore Community Hospital].

PM: And she was only a year old or so when you all moved?

FM: Eleven days.

PM: Why did you leave at that point?

FM: Her father left and I couldn't keep up the furnace and all that. So my dad came and got me.

PM: That was in 1954.

FM: Yes.

PM: Did you ever meet any other female lighthouse keepers?

FM: No. I met Pearl Pawloski. Her dad was the assistant keeper at Little Sable Point. I came to know her. I don't think I ever met any more lighthouse keepers. I went on a lighthouse tour, a bus tour, about five years ago. And the people on the bus were so delighted that they had a real lighthouse keeper on their bus. That was a lot of fun. I saw some lighthouses I hadn't seen before because they were on the other side of Lake Michigan. I had a lot of fun on that trip. But I didn't meet any light keepers.

PM: Did you realize how unique you were, being a woman in this job?

FM: Yes. It was so much fun, I wouldn't have given it up for anything.

PM: Did you get along with the men you reported to, that came on inspections?

FM: Oh, yes. I had no problem with them.

PM: They didn't treat you differently because you were a woman?

FM: No.

PM: I went out to the [White River] lighthouse before this interview and took some pictures. And there are a lot of houses along there now. Were there a lot when you were there?

FM: Well, on your right as you came down the hill, you see condominiums and none of those were there. It was just a tourist [home] where they rented rooms and furnished meals, just like where I had stayed at Sylvan Beach. And there have been several new houses built in there beside those condos. They spend money like it was water. They're all wealthy people from Chicago. Some have boats at the White Lake Yacht Club.

PM: But, when you were there, there weren't houses around there?

FM: There were older houses that had been kept up beautifully. But there weren't that many new houses.

PM: Were you lonely out at the lighthouse?

FM: The neighbors weren't there in the winter. I was pretty isolated then. But there were all kinds of people in the summer. Most of the resorters had old homes on both sides of the lake; they didn't pay attention to me because I didn't have money like they did. I made friends with those that wanted to, and those that didn't I just left them alone.

I had a good friend on the White Lake side. She was the best cook. Oh gads, could she cook! She was a colored maid for the Pierson family. Oh, she could make biscuits that would melt in your mouth. So I visited her quite often. [Laugh.]

PM: What was her name?

FM: Nancy Jordan. She looked just like Aunt Jemima! Then right next door to the lighthouse was the Flintcraft family. And they had seven kids of their own, and when they were all grown up, they had those kids' kids. I did a lot of baking for her, because she wanted fresh pie all the time. And she couldn't make pie crust. So I'd make her pie crust for that whole bunch.

Her one granddaughter was a cute girl, but she was here and there and yon so quickly. They had stairs that came up to the back door and, one day, I was halfway up the stairs with pie crusts on both my arms. And she came out the door and pie crusts went everywhere. She says, "Can't we piece them back together?" I said, "No, I believe there'd be a little sand in there!" So, I had to go home and start over. [Laugh.]

PM: I've heard that you were on the TV show *What's My Line*. How did they get your name?

FM: I knew this fellow who had a store in Pontiac, but he went to New York fairly often on buying trips. So, one time I was in Pontiac visiting my mother and he asked for a picture of me. And I said, "What do you want a picture of me for?" And he said, "Don't ask questions; just give me a picture." So I did.

One day after that, the phone rang and this girl said, "This is Barbara So-and-so from *What's My Line?* Can you be in New York next Sunday?" I said, "Good grief. Can't you give me a little more time than that?" She said, "No, you have to be here Sunday." So I said, "Yes, I'll be there somehow." She sent me the itinerary. We went on trains back then; there weren't a lot of flights going anywhere. So I took a train from Holland to Port Huron [across Canada to New York state], down the river, and into New York City. First time I'd ever taken a train on that route, so it was quite interesting.

And I was on *What's My Line?* that night.

PM: Did they guess what you did?

FM: They got in the cereal business down around Battle Creek and Kalamazoo and they couldn't seem to get out of that rut. So they never got to lighthouses at all.

PM: Did you get anything for appearing on the show?

FM: Oh yes, I got $50! But I also got a trip to New York and a room at the Hotel Edison. That was 1953.

PM: I don't think people stumped them that much. Do you remember which people were on the panel that night?

FM: Yes, there was Bennett Cerf, Dorothy Kilgallen, and...what's that dark-haired girl's name? Doris somebody...

PM: Did you hope to make a lifelong career in lighthouse keeping? If things hadn't gone bad with the marriage, do you think you would have kept at it?

FM: Yeah, I think I probably would have.

PM: What did you do after you left?

FM: I worked at different industries in the office. That's what I had trained to do was office work. I had a string of thirty-five years at Dupont in Montague, across the river.

PM: That's a lot of years. How old were you when you retired?

FM: I was sixty-eight. I didn't really want to retire, but they thought I should.

PM: Did you wear a uniform of any kind [as a keeper]?

FM: No. I never had one.

PM: Did you get much time off?

FM: Oh, no. I was on duty twenty-four hours a day, seven days a week.

PM: What if you wanted to visit your family in Pontiac?

FM: They didn't nail me down to that. I did go down there once and visited for about three days. I had Mrs. Flintcraft watch the light for me. I gave her my mother's phone number. Everything worked out okay. That was the only time I was ever gone.

PM: Did your family come to visit you?

FM: Yes, my dad and mother came, and my brother was with them. Daddy was just enthralled with that place. He went out and sat on the concrete wall by the hour. We almost had to pick him up and put him in the car to send him home! He just thought that was God's world out there. He really loved it.

PM: How many bedrooms were in the lighthouse?

FM: Downstairs there was one room that we used as a bedroom, but it was very small. And the bathroom was downstairs. Then upstairs on the side of the house opposite the tower there were two bedrooms: one big and one small. That's all there was.

PM: Two bedrooms up and one small down...

FM: And we had a big kitchen. We used to close the door between the dining room and the kitchen in the wintertime and then cook on the wood stove that was in the dining room. All the heat came from this wood stove, until they put the furnace in. We never used the upstairs at all.

PM: What other buildings were on the site? There's a little brick building there now.

FM: That was the oil and paint building. Then there was a little garage down on the corner of the building. But nobody ever used it

83

for a garage, it was so little. I don't think the door worked very good, though.

PM: Did you have a car while you were there?

FM: Oh, yeah. I had a car, but I kept it by the house.

PM: If you needed to go Muskegon, would you go by car or go by boat?

FM: I'd go by car.

PM: Did you have a TV?

FM: A couple of years before I left there, we bought a TV. Gosh we had so much [signal] snow; we put a big aerial up halfway to Timbuktu trying to pick up stations. We could get Milwaukee, and once in a while Chicago. But all the stations had a lot of snow. It wasn't much fun watching TV! [Laugh.]

PM: What did you do for entertainment then?

FM: We didn't do much. We played cards, always played pinochle.

PM: Were you a reader?

FM: Oh yes, I loved to read, read a lot, and there were a lot of books left there.

PM: Tell me about what it was like to work on Lake Michigan.

FM: [Visitors to Lake Michigan] just didn't realize the power of nature. You just couldn't tell them anything. They'd just look at you with a blank look on their face, like "What are you talking about?" You had to watch what you were doing.

PM: You mentioned the children that fell in the water from the channel walls. Did you have other life-saving situations?

FM: There was a group of women who came to the lake from Ohio every summer, and none of them could swim. And they'd jump into the water, into Lake Michigan you know, where it was so deep. And then they'd start walking out. Well, you could walk out in one place, but two feet away you couldn't because of the power of water that could dig holes in the sand.

So then they'd flap around in there for a while and try to stand up. Then they'd hit a hole and would panic. They just had no sense of anything.

PM: So you'd rescue them? You must have been a very strong swimmer.

FM: Well, I was a pretty good swimmer, but boy when you get a hold of a heavy woman and she's trying to drown you… [Laugh.] One of them had a really chunky build, and finally I had to just about knock her out and then pull her in because I couldn't do anything with her. And she said, "You hurt me." And I said, "Well, it was either that or let you die."

PM: Sounds frightening.

FM: Yeah, Lake Michigan can be a very dangerous place to be if you can't swim. And some people who get into riptides don't realize it until it's too late.

PM: Did you ever get caught in a riptide?

FM: Yes, I did. And it was no fun. You swim like crazy and you go out instead of in. I was lucky; there were some men on the beach who knew me, so I screamed and waved my hand, and they came out and pulled me in. And they said, "What were you doing in that riptide?" I said, "I didn't do it intentionally. I can certainly say that."

PM: That must have been one of your more memorable moments.

FM: Yes, it certainly was!

PM: What about good memories? What would be a good memorable moment that you had?

FM: I had lots of good times down on the beach. Picnics and hotdog roasts…

PM: With your neighbors?

FM: Yeah, and friends that came to visit me. My sister came up with her kids. We were planning on a hotdog roast, and we got one of those northwest winds. You know how they can blow in all of a sudden. And Fourth of July was like the middle of December! Gads, was it cold. But I've got pictures of us with winter jackets on sitting down on the beach roasting hotdogs over the fire. Those kids were bound and determined to roast hotdogs on the beach. So, we did! Boy, was it cold. But Lake Michigan can do that to you.

PM: What other leisure activities did you engage in? Did you have a garden at the lighthouse?

FM: We tried a garden, but that sand was all sand. [Laugh.] It didn't grow much.

PM: Did you have any livestock, any animals?

FM: No, just a dog.

PM: Did you celebrate the holidays any differently because you were at a lighthouse?

FM: Friends just came up and wanted to light fireworks out over the lake, and we let them if they wanted to.

PM: From the tower?

FM: Yeah.

PM: Did you entertain a lot inside the lighthouse?

FM: No, not a lot. We were pretty much stay-at-homes.

PM: It was a couple of miles into town, wasn't it, into White-hall?

FM: Seven miles.

PM: I see you have a photo with the lighthouse flying a flag. What day was that?

FM: That must have been July Fourth or something. I know I didn't put the flag up there. I don't do heights like that. I cleaned the light inside and out and I hung on.

PM: Thankfully, you didn't have to paint the outside of the lighthouse, that lovely brick building. Was it warm in there?

FM: Oh yes. And once you heated it up, those walls stayed warm forever.

PM: The walls were, what, about ten inches thick?

FM: Fourteen inches.

PM: Did you also have to maintain a light at the end of the channel?

FM: Oh yes, I told them I couldn't do that when I was here as a single person. Then they electrified it. But when Leo and I were first there, it was an acetylene tank [powered] light. You know how the ice builds up into a peak? We had to go out with pick axes and break up holes in the ice to put our feet in to take one step, then break another hole for another step to change the tanks on the light.

PM: How often did you have to do that?

FM: Just once in the winter, but that was enough. Gads, that was a scary trip. We roped each other together, so if one fell in we could pull on the other one. As luck would have it, none fell in. Leo was pretty strong and hacked some pretty large holes, so I could have something to put my feet in.

PM: At this light, what order lens was there? Fourth or fifth, maybe?

FM: It was a fourth order.

PM: And there was a light bulb. Just one light bulb inside?

FM: Yes, but see, the lens's glass prisms reflected all that light. And then besides that, the two sides of the light that were brass on the outside were sterling silver on the inside. And I had to keep those polished up, so they reflected the light also. [With] the light shining on those silver doors and the prisms of the light, there were two or three ways the light was magnified.

PM: What did you use to clean the glass and the brass? What kind of product?

FM: The Coast Guard furnished me with a cleaner. I don't know what it was, but it did a good job.

PM: Did you do that every day?

FM: Yes, every day.

PM: How many steps up to the top [of the tower]?

FM: I'm not sure, but the tower is 38 feet tall.

PM: Did you have to go outside to get into the tower?

FM: No. But I did go outside to clean the windows from the storms that would come in. And I'd hang on for dear life to the fence around the light.

PM: Do you remember what the lighthouse signal was?

FM: Yes, our light was ten seconds on and ten seconds off. All white.

PM: Did you have a foghorn there?

FM: No, we could hear the Muskegon one, but we didn't have one of our own.

PM: What about your laundry?

FM: I had an old Maytag washer of my own. They had two laundry tubs down there. So I washed in the Maytag tub and rinsed the clothes in the other tub, and I usually hung them outside to dry. Except when it got so cold I couldn't stand it. Then I had some lines put up in the basement and I hung them down there.

It was nice to hang sheets outside. Except when the birds— those seagulls—ate berries on the beach. They're not fit for humans to eat, but they ate them and they'd [defecate] as they flew over my sheets. Oh, God! That stuff was so hard to get out.

One day, my second husband, Herald, was out in the yard. He had a nice big ice cream cone. He'd just started to eat it and one of those birds flew over and dropped something right on top of his ice cream cone. Oh, was he mad!

PM: Did Herald enjoy life at the lighthouse?

FM: Oh yes, he enjoyed it. He didn't have to do anything either! He enjoyed fishing and just sitting on the steps of the lighthouse, looking over the scenery. He just enjoyed being there. Of course, he had a job in Muskegon, so he was home fairly early. He had a pretty soft life. [Laugh.]

PM: Do you know if you were the last woman lighthouse keeper...ever?

FM: No, I don't know. I'm sure there's still some out there.

PM: Actually, there's only one lighthouse keeper now, and that person serves at Boston Harbor. In Michigan, the last lighthouse to be staffed was Point Betsie in 1983.

Have you heard of the lighthouse historians Thomas and Phyllis Tag?

FM: Yes, I've got two of their books.

PM: The two of them have made lists of who's served at what lighthouses in Michigan, and they've identified more than fifty women who were either assistants or full-fledged keepers from the period of 1849 to the end of your period of service.

But you're one of the few in the twentieth century. By the 1920s, you didn't see women's names showing up in the records anymore. So you're unique in that aspect too.

Did you enjoy having the Coast Guard as an employer?

FM: Yes, I got along with everybody except the owners of the dog on the inspector's boat.

PM: Could you have become part of the military aspect of that? Or were you not allowed to?

FM: I suppose I could, but I didn't. They probably wouldn't have paid me any more money. [Laugh.]

PM: Did you get a retirement?

FM: No, and I don't think Leo did either. We didn't stay that long.

PM: Have there been any reunions over the years of keepers or Coast Guard personnel?

FM: Not that I'm aware of.

PM: So when you left in the 1950s, you pretty much closed the door on that part of your life.

FM: Yes. Everybody went their own way, I guess.

PM: Do you think of yourself as a pioneer?

FM: No, not really. [Laugh.]

PM: Because you were.

FM: Well, I sure enjoyed it, whatever I was.

 CHAPTER THIRTEEN

Epilogue

Did any of Michigan's Ladies of the Lights have a second act, after they concluded their light keeping careers? Age had a lot to do with that decision.

A number of female keepers were advanced in years; resignation meant their retirement from work. Among the oldest were Grace Holmes (65), Julia Brawn Way (66), Sarah Lane (67), and Elizabeth Van Riper Williams (71).

At the other end of the spectrum, Frances Wuori Johnson was only thirty-three when she retired in 1954. She moved on to a long and fulfilling career as an office manager in industry.[1]

Caroline Litogot Antaya voluntarily ended her career young—at age forty—to start a new family with her second husband. She gave birth to her fifth child and first daughter the year before she resigned.[2]

For most Michigan women, though, the record of their lives after lighthouse keeping is incomplete. After assisting her husband Stephen for five years at Gull Rock light, Mary Cocking ceases to show up in service records. It is thought that she moved with him to his next posting, Eagle Harbor, where he served until 1889. Alice Nolen followed this pattern over a decade later at the same lights.

Sarah Caswell's story is obscured by her more famous husband Burr Caswell, pioneer settler in Mason County. After their keeping years were over, she may or may not have accompanied him to Mitchell, South Dakota, to own and operate a hotel. It depends on which reference you read.[3]

In the case of widows, it is only possible to trace their whereabouts in later life if they chose not to marry again. Such was the case of Mary Ann Wheatley, whose 1906 obituary noted that she had been living in Seattle, Washington, at the time of her death.[4] The golden years of such long-serving keepers as Annie McGuire (eight years) and Mrs. William Monroe (nine years), however, are simply a question mark.

Did Michigan's Ladies of the Lights long for the life they left behind? With so little recorded history, it is difficult to know. One can only guess that some shared the sentiments of New England poet Celia Thaxter, who wrote the following stanzas in 1860 while "land-locked" on the mainland away from the lighthouse she grew up in:

Black lie the hills; swiftly doth daylight flee;
And, catching gleams of sunset's dying smile,
Through the dusk land for many a changing mile
The river runneth softly to the sea.

O happy river, could I follow thee!
O yearning heart, that never can be still!
O wistful eyes, that watch the steadfast hill,
Longing for level line of solemn sea!

Have patience; here are flowers and songs of birds,
Beauty and fragrance, wealth of sound and sight,
All summer's glory thine from morn till night,
And life too full of joy for uttered words.

Neither am I ungrateful; but I dream
Deliciously how twilight falls to-night
Over the glimmer water, how the light
Dies blissfully away, until I seem

To feel the wind, sea-scented, on my cheek,
To catch the sound of dusky flapping sail
And dip of oars, and voices on the gale
Afar off, calling low—my name they speak!

O Earth! Thy summer song of joy may soar
Ringing to heaven in triumph. I but crave
The sad, caressing murmur of the wave
That breaks in tender music on the shore.[5]

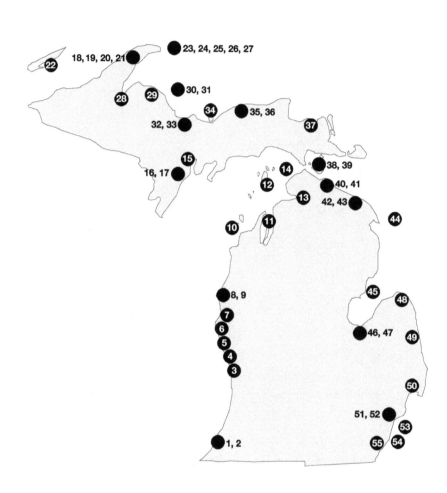

18, 19, 20, 21   23, 24, 25, 26, 27

30, 31

32, 33   34   35, 36

37

29

28

22

15

16, 17

14   38, 39

12   40, 41

13   42, 43

44

11   45

10   48

8, 9   46, 47   49

7

6

5   50

4

3   51, 52   53

55   54

1, 2

❉ GEOGRAPHICAL LIST OF KEEPERS ❉

Name	Light	Year(s)
1. Slatira Carlton	St. Joseph Light	1861
2. Jane Enos	St. Joseph Light	1876–81
3. Mrs. Harry Miller	Grand Haven Light	1872–75
4. Mrs. William Monroe	Muskegon & Pierhead Lights	1862–71
5. Frances Wuori Johnson	White River Light	1944–54
6. Mrs. H. G. Hunter	Little Sable Point Light	1910
7. Annie McGuire	Pentwater Pier Light	1877–85
8. Elsea Hyde	Big Sable Point Light	1869–71
9. Sarah Caswell	Big Sable Point Light	1874–82
10. Julia Sheridan	South Manitou Island Light	1872–78
11. Sarah Lane	Mission Point Light	1906–7
12. Elizabeth Van Riper Williams	Beaver Island Harbor Light	1872–84
13. Elizabeth Van Riper Williams	Little Traverse Light	1884–1913
14. Nancy Hume	Skillagalee Light	1869
15. Katherine Marvin	Squaw Point Light	1898–1904
16. Mary Terry	Sand Point (Escanaba) Light	1868–86
17. Mrs. Peter Peterson	Sand Point (Escanaba) Light	1913
18. Susan Bennetts	Portage Lake Ship Canal Light	1907
19. Julia Ann Griswold	Eagle River Light	1861–65
20. Mary Ann Wheatley	Eagle Harbor Range Lights	1898–1905
21. Mrs. C. E. Thomson	Eagle Harbor Range Lights	1905
22. M. A. Stevens	Menagerie Island Light	1875–78
23. Mary Cocking	Gull Rock Light	1872–77
24. Mary Corgan	Gull Rock Light	1877–83
25. Alice Nolen	Gull Rock Light	1892–1903
26. Lydia Smith	Manitou Island Light	1855–56
27. Mary Corgan	Manitou Island Light	1873–75
28. Anne Crebassa	Sand Point (Baraga) Light	1908
29. Jennie Beamer	Big Bay Point Light	1898
30. Rozella Wilson	Granite Island Light	1873–76
31. Anna Carlson	Granite Island Light	1903

32. Anastasia Truckey	Marquette Harbor Light	1862–65
33. Catharine McGuire	Marquette Harbor Light	1882–91
34. Mrs. H. Lubuck	Grand Island East Channel Light	1862–65
35. Mary Beedon	Au Sable Point Light	1876–79
36. Mary Gigandet	Au Sable Point Light	1892–97
37. Mrs. Donald Harrison	St. Mary's River Range Light	1902
38. Mrs. Charles O'Malley	Bois Blanc Island Light	1854–55
39. Mary Granger	Bois Blanc Island Light	1857
40. Jane Barr	Cheboygan Crib Light	1879–80
41. Mrs. Ivory Littlefield	Cheboygan River Range Light	1894
42. Mary Garraty	New Presque Isle Light	1872–82
43. Anna Garraty	Presque Isle Harbor Range Lights	1903–26
44. Catharine McGuire	Thunder Bay Island Light	1874–82
45. Harriet Howard	Charity Island Light	1877–79
46. Julia Brawn Way	Saginaw River Lights	1873–82
47. Nellie Buzzard	Saginaw River Lights	1883–86
48. Catherine Shook	Pointe aux Barques Light	1849–51
49. Grace Holmes	Port Sanilac Light	1926–28
50. Caroline Warner	St. Clair Flats South Channel Range Lights	1882–92
51. Lucy Gramer	Ecorse Range Light	1898
52. Mary Gramer	Ecorse Range Light	1906
53. Jane Knapp	Grassy Island South Light	1880–84
54. Caroline Litogot Antaya	Mamajuda Light	1874–85
55. Mary Vreeland	Gibraltar Light	1876–79

✳ ALPHABETICAL LIST OF KEEPERS BY LAST NAME ✳

Note: The designations AK (for assistant keeper) and K (for keeper) reflect the highest job level each woman attained.

Name	Light	Year(s)
Antaya, Caroline Litogot (K)	Mamajuda Light	1874–85
Barr, Jane (K)	Cheboygan Crib Light	1879–80
Beamer, Jennie (AK)	Big Bay Point Light	1898
Beedon, Mary (AK)	Au Sable Point Light	1876–79
Bennetts, Susan (AK)	Portage Lake Ship Canal Light	1907
Buzzard, Nellie (AK)	Saginaw River Lights	1883–86
Carlson, Anna (AK)	Granite Island Light	1903
Carlton, Slatira (K)	St. Joseph Light	1861
Caswell, Sarah (AK)	Big Sable Point Light	1874–82
Cocking, Mary (AK)	Gull Rock Light	1872–77
Corgan, Mary (AK, AK)	Manitou Island Light	1873–75
	Gull Rock Light	1877–83
Crebassa, Anne (AK)	Sand Point (Baraga) Light	1908
Enos, Jane (K)	St. Joseph Light	1876–81
Garraty, Anna (K)	Presque Isle Harbor Range Lights	1903–26
Garraty, Mary (AK)	New Presque Isle Light	1872–82
Gigandet, Mary (AK)	Au Sable Point Light	1892–97
Gramer, Lucy (K)	Ecorse Range Light	1898
Gramer, Mary (K)	Ecorse Range Light	1906
Granger, Mary (K)	Bois Blanc Island Light	1857
Griswold, Julia Ann (K)	Eagle River Light	1861–65
Harrison, Mrs. Donald (K)	St. Mary's River Range Light	1902
Holmes, Grace (K)	Port Sanilac Light	1926–28
Howard, Harriet (AK)	Charity Island Light	1877–79
Hume, Nancy (AK)	Skillagalee Light	1869
Hunter, Mrs. H. G. (K)	Little Sable Point Light	1910
Hyde, Elsea (AK)	Big Sable Point Light	1869–71
Johnson, Frances Wuori (K)	White River Light	1944–54

Knapp, Jane (K)	Grassy Island South Light	1880–84
Lane, Sarah (K)	Mission Point Light	1906–7
Littlefield, Mrs. Ivory (K)	Cheboygan River Range Light	1894
Lubuck, Mrs. H. (AK)	Grand Island East Channel Light	1862–65
Marvin, Katherine (K)	Squaw Point Light	1898–1904
McGuire, Annie (K)	Pentwater Pier Light	1877–85
McGuire, Catharine (AK, AK)	Thunder Bay Island Light	1874–82
	Marquette Harbor Light	1882–91
Miller, Mrs. Harry (AK)	Grand Haven Light	1872–75
Monroe, Mrs. William (K)	Muskegon & Pierhead Lights	1862–71
Nolen, Alice (AK)	Gull Rock Light	1892–1903
O'Malley, Mrs. Charles (K)	Bois Blanc Island Light	1854–55
Peterson, Mrs. Peter (K)	Sand Point (Escanaba) Light	1913
Sheridan, Julia (AK)	South Manitou Island Light	1872–78
Shook, Catherine (K)	Pointe aux Barques Light	1849–51
Smith, Lydia (AK)	Manitou Island Light	1855–56
Stevens, M. A. (AK)	Menagerie Island Light	1875–78
Terry, Mary (K)	Sand Point (Escanaba) Light	1868–86
Thomson, Mrs. C. E. (K)	Eagle Harbor Range Lights	1905
Truckey, Anastasia (K)	Marquette Harbor Light	1862–65
Vreeland, Mary (K)	Gibraltar Light	1876–79
Warner, Caroline (AK)	St. Clair Flats South Channel Range Lights	1882–92
Way, Julia Brawn (K)	Saginaw River Lights	1873–82
Wheatley, Mary Ann (K)	Eagle Harbor Range Lights	1898–1905
Williams, Elizabeth Van Riper (K, K)	Beaver Island Harbor Light	1872–84
	Little Traverse Light	1884–1913
Wilson, Rozella (AK)	Granite Island Light	1873–76

✳ ALPHABETICAL LIST OF KEEPERS BY LIGHTHOUSE ✳

Light	Name	Year(s)
Au Sable Point Light	Mary Beedon	1876–79
	Mary Gigandet	1892–97
Beaver Island Harbor Light	Elizabeth Van Riper Williams	1872–84
Big Bay Point Light	Jennie Beamer	1898
Big Sable Point Light	Elsea Hyde	1869–71
	Sarah Caswell	1874–82
Bois Blanc Island Light	Mrs. Charles O'Malley	1854–55
	Mary Granger	1857
Charity Island Light	Harriet Howard	1877–79
Cheboygan Crib Light	Jane Barr	1879–80
Cheboygan River Range Light	Mrs. Ivory Littlefield	1894
Eagle Harbor Range Lights	Mary Ann Wheatley	1898–1905
	Mrs. C. E. Thomson	1905
Eagle River Light	Julia Ann Griswold	1861–65
Ecorse Range Light	Lucy Gramer	1898
	Mary Gramer	1906
Gibraltar Light	Mary Vreeland	1876–79
Grand Haven Light	Mrs. Harry Miller	1872–75
Grand Island East Channel Light	Mrs. H. Lubuck	1862–65
Granite Island Light	Rozella Wilson	1873–76
	Anna Carlson	1903
Grassy Island South Light	Jane Knapp	1880–84
Gull Rock Light	Mary Cocking	1872–77
	Mary Corgan	1877–83
	Alice Nolen	1892–1903
Little Sable Point Light	Mrs. H. G. Hunter	1910
Little Traverse Light	Elizabeth Van Riper Williams	1884–1913
Mamajuda Light	Caroline Litogot Antaya	1874–85
Manitou Island Light	Lydia Smith	1855–56
	Mary Corgan	1873–75

Marquette Harbor Light	Anastasia Truckey	1862–65
	Catharine McGuire	1882–91
Menagerie Island Light	M. A. Stevens	1875–78
Mission Point Light	Sarah Lane	1906–7
Muskegon & Pierhead Lights	Mrs. William Monroe	1862–71
New Presque Isle Light	Mary Garraty	1872–82
Pentwater Pier Light	Annie McGuire	1877–85
Pointe aux Barques Light	Catherine Shook	1849–51
Port Sanilac Light	Grace Holmes	1926–28
Portage Lake Ship Canal Light	Susan Bennetts	1907
Presque Isle Harbor Range Lights	Anna Garraty	1903–26
Saginaw River Lights	Julia Brawn Way	1873–82
	Nellie Buzzard	1883–86
Sand Point (Baraga) Light	Anne Crebassa	1908
Sand Point (Escanaba) Light	Mary Terry	1868–86
	Mrs. Peter Peterson	1913
Skillagalee Light	Nancy Hume	1869
South Manitou Island Light	Julia Sheridan	1872–78
Squaw Point Light	Katherine Marvin	1898–1904
St. Clair Flats South Channel Range Lights	Caroline Warner	1882–92
St. Joseph Light	Slatira Carlton	1861
	Jane Enos	1876–81
St. Mary's River Range Light	Mrs. Donald Harrison	1902
Thunder Bay Island Light	Catharine McGuire	1874–82
White River Light	Frances Wuori Johnson	1944–54

✳ CHRONOLOGICAL LIST OF KEEPERS ✳

Year(s)	Name	Light
1849–51	Catherine Shook	Pointe aux Barques Light
1854–55	Mrs. Charles O'Malley	Bois Blanc Island Light
1855–56	Lydia Smith	Manitou Island Light
1857	Mary Granger	Bois Blanc Island Light
1861	Slatira Carlton	St. Joseph Light
1861–65	Julia Ann Griswold	Eagle River Light
1862–65	Mrs. H. Lubuck	Grand Island East Channel Light
1862–65	Anastasia Truckey	Marquette Harbor Light
1862–71	Mrs. William Monroe	Muskegon & Pierhead Lights
1868–86	Mary Terry	Sand Point (Escanaba) Light
1869	Nancy Hume	Skillagalee Light
1869–71	Elsea Hyde	Big Sable Point Light
1872–75	Mrs. Harry Miller	Grand Haven Light
1872–77	Mary Cocking	Gull Rock Light
1872–78	Julia Sheridan	South Manitou Island Light
1872–82	Mary Garraty	New Presque Isle Light
1872–84	Elizabeth Van Riper Williams	Beaver Island Harbor Light
1873–75	Mary Corgan	Manitou Island Light
1873–76	Rozella Wilson	Granite Island Light
1873–82	Julia Brawn Way	Saginaw River Lights
1874–82	Sarah Caswell	Big Sable Point Light
1874–82	Catharine McGuire	Thunder Bay Island Light
1874–85	Caroline Litogot Antaya	Mamajuda Light
1875–78	M. A. Stevens	Menagerie Island Light
1876–79	Mary Vreeland	Gibraltar Light
1876–81	Jane Enos	St. Joseph Light
1876–79	Mary Beedon	Au Sable Point Light
1877–79	Harriet Howard	Charity Island Light
1877–83	Mary Corgan	Gull Rock Light
1877–85	Annie McGuire	Pentwater Pier Light
1879–80	Jane Barr	Cheboygan Crib Light

1880–84	Jane Knapp	Grassy Island South Light
1882–91	Catharine McGuire	Marquette Harbor Light
1882–92	Caroline Warner	St. Clair Flats South Channel Range Lights
1883–86	Nellie Buzzard	Saginaw River Lights
1884–1913	Elizabeth Van Riper Williams	Little Traverse Light
1892–97	Mary Gigandet	Au Sable Point Light
1892–1903	Alice Nolen	Gull Rock Light
1894	Mrs. Ivory Littlefield	Cheboygan River Range Light
1898–1904	Katherine Marvin	Squaw Point Light
1898–1905	Mary Ann Wheatley	Eagle Harbor Range Lights
1898	Jennie Beamer	Big Bay Point Light
1898	Lucy Gramer	Ecorse Range Light
1902	Mrs. Donald Harrison	St. Mary's River Range Light
1903	Anna Carlson	Granite Island Light
1903–26	Anna Garraty	Presque Isle Harbor Range Lights
1905	Mrs. C. E. Thomson	Eagle Harbor Range Lights
1906	Mary Gramer	Ecorse Range Light
1906–7	Sarah Lane	Mission Point Light
1907	Susan Bennetts	Portage Lake Ship Canal Light
1908	Anne Crebassa	Sand Point (Baraga) Light
1910	Mrs. H. G. Hunter	Little Sable Point Light
1913	Mrs. Peter Peterson	Sand Point (Escanaba) Light
1926–28	Grace Holmes	Port Sanilac Light
1944–54	Frances Wuori Johnson	White River Light

✳ SUGGESTED READING ✳

Want to learn more about Michigan women in the U.S. Lighthouse Service? The following books and websites can help.

ADULT BOOKS

A Child of the Sea; and Life among the Mormons. Elizabeth Whitney Williams. St. James, MI: Henry Allen, 1905.

Guardians of the Lights: The Men and Women of the U.S. Lighthouse Service. Elinor DeWire. Sarasota, FL: Pineapple Press, 1995.

Women Who Kept the Lights: An Illustrated History of Female Lighthouse Keepers. Mary Louise Clifford and J. Candace Clifford. Alexandria, VA: Cypress Communications, 2000.

The Women's Great Lakes Reader. Victoria Brehm. Tustin, MI: Ladyslipper Press, 2000.

CHILDREN'S BOOKS (NONFICTION)

Elizabeth Whitney Williams and the Little Traverse Light. Mary Hramiec Hoffman. Harbor Springs, MI: Hramiec Hoffman Publishing, 2004.

Lighthouses for Kids: History, Science, and Lore with 21 Activities. Katherine L. House. Chicago: Chicago Review Press, 2008.

Mind the Light, Katie: The History of Thirty-Three Female Lighthouse Keepers. Mary Louise Clifford and J. Candace Clifford (a children's version of their *Women Who Kept the Lights*). Alexandria, VA: Cypress Communications, 2006.

CHILDREN'S BOOKS (FICTION)

Finding My Light. Chris Shanley-Dillman. Frederick, MD: PublishAmerica, 2006.

To Keep the South Manitou Light. Anna Egan Smucker. Detroit: Wayne State University Press, 2005.

Keeper of the Light. Patricia Curtis Pfitsch. New York: Simon & Schuster Books for Young Readers, 1997.

MAGAZINES

Lighthouse Digest, published by Lighthouse Depot, Wells, Maine.

WEBSITES

Keeper of the Light (an online book about Elizabeth Van Riper Williams), http://www.americanepic.org/keeperofthelight.

National Park Service Maritime Heritage Program/Keepers as Heroes, http://www.nps.gov/history/maritime/keep/keephero.htm.

Seeing the Light: Lighthouses of the Western Great Lakes, http://www.terrypepper.com/lights/index.htm.

U.S. Coast Guard/Breaking the Barrier: Women Lighthouse Keepers and Other Female Employees of the U.S. Lighthouse Board/Service, http://www.uscg.mil/history/Women_Keepers.html.

⁂ NOTES ⁂

CHAPTER 1

1. Francis Ross Holland, *America's Lighthouses: An Illustrated History* (New York: Dover, 1988), 9.

2. Mary Louise Clifford and J. Candace Clifford, *Women Who Kept the Lights: An Illustrated History of Female Lighthouse Keepers*, 2nd ed. (Alexandria: Cypress Communications, 2000), 5.

3. Francis Ross Holland, *Lighthouses* (New York: Metro, 1995), 15.

4. "Youghal," *The Commissioners of Irish Lights*, http://www.cil.ie/flat_areaEQLlighthousesAMPlighthouseIDEQL20_entry.html (accessed April 12, 2009).

5. Holland, 178.

6. Ohio Department of Natural Resources, "Marblehead Lighthouse," *Ohio State Parks*, http://www.dnr.state.oh.us/parks/magazinehome/mag1998fallwin/marbleheadfw1998/tabid/393/default.aspx (accessed April 12, 2009).

7. Charles K. Hyde, *The Northern Lights: Lighthouses of the Upper Great Lakes*, rev. ed. (Detroit: Wayne State University Press, 1995), 15.

8. Clifford and Clifford, 218.

9. Terry Pepper, "Bois Blanc Lighthouse," *Seeing the Light: Lighthouses of the Western Great Lakes*, http://www.terrypepper.com/lights/huron/boisblanc/keepers.htm (accessed February 22, 2007).

10. U.S. Light-House Establishment, *Compilation of Public Documents and Extracts from Reports and Papers Relating to Light-Houses, Light-Vessels, and Illuminating Apparatus, and to Beacons, Buoys, and Fog Signals, 1789–1871* (Washington, DC: Government Printing Office, 1871).

11. Clifford and Clifford, 129.

CHAPTER 2

1. "Light Stations Remaining in the United States," *U.S. Coast Guard*, http://www.uscg.mil/history/articles/h_remaininglights.asp (accessed April 5, 2009).

2. Clifford and Clifford, 209.

3. Correspondence with J. Candace Clifford, April 5, 2009.

4. Correspondence with Gladys Beckwith, April 5, 2009.

5. Elinor DeWire, *Guardians of the Lights: The Men and Women of the U.S. Lighthouse Service* (Sarasota, FL: Pineapple Press, 1995), 188.

6. "Great Lakes Lighthouses," Northern Michigan University Center for Upper Peninsula Studies, http://webb.nmu.edu/Centers/UpperPeninsulaStudies/SiteSections/UPHistory/FolkloreHistory/Lighthouses.shtml, accessed June 9, 2009.

7. Pepper, "Gull Rock Lighthouse," *Seeing the Light: Lighthouses of the Western Great Lakes*, http://www.terrypepper.com/lights/superior/gull-rock/index.htm (accessed February 22, 2007).

CHAPTER 3

1. Stephen Pleasonton, *Instructions to the Keepers of Light-Houses within the United States* (Washington, DC: Government Printing Office, 1835).

2. Holland, 15.

3. Holland, 21.

4. "Beacon to Sailors Cared for by Woman," *Grand Rapids Evening Press*, November 18, 1905.

5. Pepper, "Marquette Harbor Lighthouse," *Seeing the Light: Lighthouses of the Western Great Lakes*, http://www.terrypepper.com/lights/superior/marquette/marquette.htm (accessed February 22, 2007).

6. Holland, 45.

7. Pleasonton.

8. Richard Clayton, "John Nolen's Journal," *Lighthouse Digest*, August 1999.

9. Pleasonton.

10. Frances (Wuori Johnson) Marshall interview, in the collection of the Great Lakes Lighthouse Keepers Association, conducted December 16, 2007.

CHAPTER 4

1. Holland, 40.

2. U.S. Light-House Establishment, *Rules, Regulations, and General Instructions* (Washington, DC: William A. Harris, Printer, 1858), 8.

3. Clifford and Clifford, 129.

4. Pepper, "Eagle Harbor Range Lights," *Seeing the Light: Lighthouses of the Western Great Lakes*, http://www.terrypepper.com/lights/superior/eaglerange/eaglerange.htm (accessed February 22, 2007).

5. Pepper, "Marquette Harbor Lighthouse."

6. Marshall.

7. Pepper, "Big Bay Point Lighthouse: The Story of William H. Pryor," *Seeing the Light: Lighthouses of the Western Great Lakes*, http://www.terrypepper.com/lights/superior/bigbay/priorstory.htm (accessed February 22, 2007).

CHAPTER 5

1. Frederick Stonehouse, *Women and the Lakes: Untold Great Lakes Maritime Tales* (Gwinn, MI: Avery Color Studios, 2001), 76.

2. Sharon Gill Vanden Bossche, "Stephen A. Warner: St. Clair, MI Lighthouse Keeper," *GenForum*, http://genforum.genealogy.com/warner/messages/3074.html (accessed January 27, 2009).

3. Hyde, 52.

4. Elizabeth Whitney Williams, *A Child of the Sea; and Life among the Mormons* (St. James, MI: Henry Allen, 1905), 213.

5. David W. Landemann, *A Historical Study of the Pointe Aux Barques Lighthouse* (Grand Rapids, MI: Williams & Works, 1982), 8.

6. National Archives, Record Group 26, Entry 82.

7. Clayton.

8. Williams, 215.

CHAPTER 6

1. Unpublished manuscript on Anastasia Truckey, authored by descendant Robert L. Shanley Sr., October 30, 2001.

2. Pepper, "Menagerie Island Lighthouse," *Seeing the Light: Lighthouses of the Western Great Lakes*, http://www.terrypepper.com/lights/superior/menagerie/index.htm (accessed February 22, 2007).

3. "Great Lakes Lighthouses," Northern Michigan University Center for Upper Peninsula Studies, http://webb.nmu.edu/Centers/UpperPeninsulaStudies/SiteSectons/UPHistory/FolkloreHistory/Lighthouse.shtml (accessed June 4, 2009).

4. "Great Lakes Lighthouses."

5. "1849 Letter Concerning Fire at Keeper's Dwelling," *Pointe aux Barques Lighthouse Society*, www.pointeauxbarqueslighthouse.org/light/keepers/shookletter.cfm (accessed September 5, 2007).

6. "Great Lakes Lighthouses."

7. *Grace Holmes' Journal*, Port Sanilac, June 13, 1924.

8. Sandra L. Planisek, *Reliving Lighthouse Memories: 1930s–1970s* (Mackinaw City, MI: Great Lakes Lighthouse Keepers Association, 2004), 96.

9. DeWire, 37.

CHAPTER 7

1. Cheryl Shelton-Roberts and Bruce Roberts, *Lighthouse Families* (Birmingham, AL: Crane Hill, 1997), 50.
2. LuAnne Gaykowski Kozma, ed., *Living at a Lighthouse: Oral Histories from the Great Lakes* (Allen Park, MI: Great Lakes Lighthouse Keepers Association, 1987), 36.
3. Holland, 47.
4. Holland, 50.
5. Holland, 48.

CHAPTER 8

1. National Archives, Record Group 26, Entry 83.
2. Frederick Stonehouse, *Women and the Lakes II* (Gwinn, MI: Avery Color Studios, 2005), 135.
3. Hyde, 57.
4. H. C. Ackeley, Superintendent of Lights, Custom House, Grand Haven, Mich. to Prof. Joseph Henry, Chairman, Light-House Board, Washington, DC, March 19, 1874.
5. Holland, 45.

CHAPTER 9

1. Hyde, 56.
2. Kozma, 53.
3. John Penrod and the Great Lakes Shipwreck Historical Society, *Whitefish Point Light Station: Michigan's Most Famous Lighthouse* (Berrien Center, MI: Penrod/Hiawatha, 1998), 21.
4. Kozma, 99.
5. Kozma, 55.
6. "Michigan Historical Museum System: Copper Harbor Lighthouse," *Michigan Department of History, Arts and Libraries,* http://www.hal.state.mi.us/mhc/museum/musewil/keeping.html (accessed June 4, 2009).
7. "Beacon to Sailors Cared for by Woman."
8. "Beacon to Sailors Cared for by Woman."
9. *Memorial Record of the Northern Peninsula of Michigan* (Chicago: Lewis, 1895), 447.
10. Hyde, 53.
11. Hyde, 54.

12. Frances B. Hurlburt, "The Fall of the Lighthouse," *Grandmother's Stories* (Cambridge, MA: Riverside, 1889).

13. Pepper, "Big Bay Point Lighthouse."

14. John B. Mansfield, ed., *History of the Great Lakes, Volume II* (Chicago: J. H. Beers, 1899), 471.

15. Donald Nelson, "First Woman Lightkeeper on the Keweenaw Peninsula," *Lighthouse Digest*, March 2002.

CHAPTER 10

1. Clifford and Clifford, 103.

2. Clifford and Clifford, 63.

3. Clifford and Clifford, 13.

4. Clifford and Clifford, 202.

5. Ray Jones, *The Lighthouse Encyclopedia: The Definitive Reference* (Guilford, CT: Globe Pequot, 2004), 43.

CHAPTER 11

1. Catherine Shook's Michigan Women's Hall of Fame nomination form, authored by Deborah Eleson, February 2, 2005.

2. "Dr. Heath Drowned," *Buffalo Commercial Advertiser*, April 23, 1849.

3. Eleson.

4. "1849 Letter Concerning Fire at Keeper's Dwelling."

5. Shanley.

6. Shanley.

7. Stonehouse, *Women and the Lakes II*, 133.

8. Stonehouse, *Women and the Lakes II*, 133.

9. *History of the Upper Peninsula of Michigan* (Chicago: Western Historical, 1883), 246.

10. Unpublished manuscript on Mary Terry and Mrs. Peter Peterson, authored by Richard Stratton, undated.

11. Stratton.

12. Kathy Mason, "Mystery at Sand Point Lighthouse," *Michigan History*, September/October 2003, 24.

13. Mason, 24.

14. Mason, 25.

15. "Aaron Sheridan," *National Park Service/Sleeping Bear Dunes National Lakeshore*, www.nps.gov/slbe/planyourvisit/aaronsheridan.htm (accessed January 8, 2009).

16. Harold and Linda Saffron, "Leelanau County MI Archives Photo Tombstone: Sheridan, Julia Moore and Robert R." *USGen Web Archives.* http://files.us gwarchives.net/mi/leelanau/photos/tombstones/southmanitouisla/sheri dan135687gph.txt (accessed January 8, 2009).

17. *Traverse City Eagle-Herald*, March 21, 1878.

18. Christina Campbell, "Mystery, Madness and Intrigue in the Manitou Passage," *Glen Arbor Sun*, July 31, 2003.

19. www.nps.gov/slbe/planyourvisit/aaronsheridan.htm (accessed January 8, 2009).

20. "Mrs. Garrity Dies, Aged 80," *Alpena Evening News*, December 30, 1912.

21. Pepper, "New Presque Isle Lighthouse," *Seeing the Light: Lighthouses of the Western Great Lakes*, http://www.terrypepper.com/lights/huron/newpresqisl/in dex.htm (accessed February 22, 2007).

22. "Mrs. Garrity Dies, Aged 80."

23. Williams, biography page.

24. Williams, 65.

25. Williams, 142.

26. Williams, 208.

27. Williams, 213.

28. Williams, 215.

29. Williams, 224.

30. Williams, 228.

31. Williams, 229.

32. "Aged Charlevoix Couple Succumbs," *Charlevoix Courier*, January 26, 1938.

33. Joan Totten Musinski Rezmer, ed., *Women of Bay County: 1809–1980* (Bay City, MI: Museum of the Great Lakes, 1980), 6.

34. Pepper, "Saginaw Bay Lighthouse," *Seeing the Light: Lighthouses of the Western Great Lakes*, http://www.terrypepper.com/lights/huron/saginaw-bay/in dex.htm (accessed February 22, 2007).

35. Kantzler Maritime Gallery exhibit text relating to Julia Brawn Way, Bay County (MI) Historical Museum, undated.

36. *Memorial Record of the Northern Peninsula of Michigan* (Chicago: Lewis, 1895), 447.

37. "Keweenaw Child Born on Steam Launch in 1875," *Navy Times*, undated.

38. *Ontonagon Herald*, February 12, 1893.

39. Michael Forand, "Mamajuda Light," *Lighthouse Depot*, http://www.light housedepot.com/lite_explorer.asp?action=display_details&LighthouseID=2824 (accessed January 8, 2009).

40. Jeff Barr, "Readers Unearth a Grave Mystery," *Wyandotte News Herald*, July 1995.

41. Ford R. Bryan, *Friends, Families and Forays: Scenes from the Life and Times of Henry Ford* (Dearborn: Ford Books, 2002), 129.

42. Clifford and Clifford, 182.

43. Clifford and Clifford, 184.

44. Bryan, 130.

45. "The Litogot Family," unpublished manuscript in the collection of the Benson Ford Research Center, Dearborn, MI, undated.

46. 1860 United States Federal Census, Pipestone Township, Berrien County, MI, 151.

47. Correspondence with Christina Hirn Arseneau, the Heritage Museum and Cultural Center, St. Joseph, MI, November 20, 2007.

48. 1880 United States Federal Census, St. Joseph, Berrien County, MI, 30.

49. "St. Joseph's Lighthouse," unpublished manuscript in the collection of the Maud Preston Palenske Memorial Library, St. Joseph, MI, undated.

50. *St. Joseph Traveler Herald*, April 2, 1881.

51. 1900 United States Federal Census, Ecorse Township, Wayne County, MI, 82.

52. Kathy Covert Warnes, "The Colorful Career of Gus Gramer: Soldier, Fireman, Oarsman, and Lighthouse Person," *Lighthouse Digest*, August 2007.

53. Warnes.

54. 1900 United States Federal Census, Ecorse Township, 82.

55. "A Noble Act: Gus Gramer Willing His Wife Should Wed Again," *Wyandotte Herald*, August 24, 1900 (reprinted from the *Detroit Tribune*).

56. "A Noble Act."

57. Phyllis L. Tag and Thomas A. Tag, *The Lighthouse Keepers of Lake Erie Including Detroit River* (Dayton, OH: Great Lakes Lighthouse Research, 1998).

58. Luther Barrett, "A Successful Woman Lighthouse Keeper," *Delta Historian*, July 1985.

59. Barrett.

60. 1900 United States Federal Census, Bay de Noc Township, Delta County, MI, 32.

61. Barrett.

62. Barrett.

63. DeWire, 41.

64. Hyde, 53.

65. Patrick Garraty, *U.S. Lighthouse Service Logbook*, June 19, 1889.

66. *Presque Isle County Advance*, June 20, 1889.

67. Carol Lewis, "Mission Point Lighthouse: Lightkeeping on the Great Lakes with Sarah and John Lane," *Echoes: Newsletter of the Old Mission Peninsula Historical Society*, April 2007.

68. Lewis.

69. "Beacon to Sailors Cared for by Woman."

70. "Beacon to Sailors Cared for by Woman."

71. *History of St. Clair County, Michigan* (Chicago: A.T. Andreas, 1883), 594.

72. Correspondence with Cathi Bulone Campbell, June 4, 2009.

73. Cathi Bulone Campbell.
74. Cathi Bulone Campbell.
75. Cathi Bulone Campbell.
76. *Grace Holmes' Journal*, January 16–19, 1911.
77. Marshall.
78. Marshall.
79. Marshall.
80. Marshall.
81. Marshall.
82. De Wire, 190.

CHAPTER 13

1. Marshall.
2. 1900 United States Federal Census, Detroit, Wayne County, MI, 318.
3. "Burr Caswell," *Great Lakes History Companion*, http://ludingtonmichigan.net/burrcaswell.htm (accessed June 13, 2010).
4. "Died in the West," *Daily Mining Journal*, May 22, 1906.
5. "Seacoast Women," *Seacoast New Hampshire and South Coast Maine*, http://www.seacostnh.com/poems/celia2.html (accessed January 25, 2009).

✻ BIBLIOGRAPHY ✻

"1849 Letter Concerning Fire at Keeper's Dwelling." *Pointe aux Barques Lighthouse Society.* http://www.pointeauxbarqueslighthouse.org/light/keepers/shookletter.cfm (accessed September 5, 2007).

"A Noble Act: Gus Gramer Willing His Wife Should Wed Again." *Wyandotte Herald,* August 24, 1900 (reprinted from the *Detroit Tribune*).

"Aaron Sheridan." *National Park Service/Sleeping Bear Dunes National Lakeshore.* http://www.nps.gov/slbe/planyourvisit/aaronsheridan.htm (accessed January 8, 2009).

Ackley, H. C., Superintendent of Lights, Custom House, Grand Haven, MI, to Prof. Joseph Henry, Chairman, Light-House Board, Washington, DC, March 19, 1874.

"Aged Charlevoix Couple Succumbs." *Charlevoix Courier,* January 26, 1938.

Barr, Jeff. "Readers Unearth a Grave Mystery." *Wyandotte News Herald,* July 1995.

Barrett, Luther. "A Successful Woman Lighthouse Keeper." *Delta Historian,* July 1985.

Bay County (MI) Historical Museum Kantzler Maritime Gallery. Exhibit text relating to Julia Brawn Way, undated.

"Beacon to Sailors Cared for by Woman." *Grand Rapids Evening Press,* November 18, 1905.

Bryan, Ford R. *Friends, Families and Forays: Scenes from the Life and Times of Henry Ford.* Dearborn: Ford Books, 2002.

"Burr Caswell." *Great Lakes History Companion,* http//ludingtonmichigan.net/burrcaswell.htm (accessed June 13, 2010).

Campbell, Christina. "Mystery, Madness and Intrigue in the Manitou Passage." *Glen Arbor Sun,* July 31, 2003.

Clayton, Richard. "John Nolen's Journal." *Lighthouse Digest,* August 1999.

Clifford, Mary Louise, and J. Candace Clifford. *Women Who Kept the Lights: An Illustrated History of Female Lighthouse Keepers,* 2nd ed. Alexandria: Cypress Communications, 2000.

Correspondence with Christina Hirn Arseneau, curator, Heritage Museum and Cultural Center, St. Joseph, MI, November 20, 2007.

Correspondence with Gladys Beckwith, founder, Michigan Women's Historical Center and Hall of Fame, Lansing, MI, April 5, 2009.

Correspondence with Cathi Bulone Campbell, local historian, Port Sanilac, MI, June 4, 2009.

Correspondence with J. Candace Clifford, co-author, *Women Who Kept the Lights: An Illustrated History of Female Lighthouse Keepers*, April 5, 2009.

DeWire, Elinor. *Guardians of the Lights: The Men and Women of the U.S. Lighthouse Service*. Sarasota, FL: Pineapple Press, 1995.

"Died in the West." *Daily Mining Journal*, May 22, 1906.

"Dr. Heath Drowned." *Buffalo Commercial Advertiser*, April 23, 1849.

Eleson, Deborah. *Michigan Women's Hall of Fame Nomination: Catherine Shook.* February 21, 2005.

Forand, Michael. "Mamajuda Light." *Lighthouse Depot.* http://www.lighthousedepot.com/lite_explorer.asp?action=display_details&LighthouseID=2824 (accessed January 8, 2009).

Garraty, Patrick. *U.S. Lighthouse Service Logbook*, June 19, 1889.

Grace Holmes' Journal. Port Sanilac, January 16–19, 1911; June 13, 1924.

"Great Lakes Lighthouses." Northern Michigan University Center for Upper Peninsula Studies. http://webb.nmu.edu/Centers/UpperPeninsulaStudies/SiteSections/UPHistory/FolkloreHistory/Lighthouses.shtml (accessed June 9, 2009).

History of St. Clair County, Michigan. Chicago: A. T. Andreas, 1883.

History of the Upper Peninsula of Michigan. Chicago: Western Historical, 1883.

Holland, Francis Ross. *Lighthouses*. New York: Metro, 1995.

Holland, Francis Ross. *America's Lighthouses: An Illustrated History*. New York: Dover, 1988.

Hurlburt, Frances B. "The Fall of the Lighthouse." *Grandmother's Stories*. Cambridge: Riverside, 1889.

Hyde, Charles K. *The Northern Lights: Lighthouses of the Upper Great Lakes*, rev. ed. Detroit: Wayne State University Press, 1995.

Interview with Frances (Wuori Johnson) Marshall, former White River lighthouse keeper, in the collection of the Great Lakes Lighthouse Keepers Association, Mackinaw City, MI, conducted December 16, 2007.

Jones, Ray. *The Lighthouse Encyclopedia: The Definitive Reference*. Guilford, CT: Globe Pequot, 2004.

"Keweenaw Child Born on Steam Launch in 1875." *Navy Times*, undated.

Kozma, LuAnne Gaykowski, ed. *Living at a Lighthouse: Oral Histories from the Great Lakes*. Allen Park, MI: Great Lakes Lighthouse Keepers Association, 1987.

Landemann, David W. *A Historical Study of the Pointe aux Barques Lighthouse*. Grand Rapids: Williams & Works, 1982.

Lewis, Carol. "Mission Point Lighthouse: Lightkeeping on the Great Lakes with Sarah and John Lane." *Echoes: Newsletter of the Old Mission Peninsula Historical Society*, April 2007.

"Light Stations Remaining in the United States." *U.S. Coast Guard.* http://www uscg.mil/history/articles/h_remaininglights.asp (accessed April 5, 2009).

"The Litogot Family." Unpublished manuscript in the collection of the Benson Ford Research Center, Dearborn, MI, undated.

Mansfield, John B., ed. *History of the Great Lakes, Volume II.* Chicago: J. H. Beers, 1899.

Mason, Kathy. "Mystery at Sand Point Lighthouse." *Michigan History*, September/October 2003.

"Michigan Historical Museum System: Copper Harbor Lighthouse." *Michigan Department of History, Arts and Libraries.* http://www.hal.state.mi.us/mhc/museum/musewil/keeping.html (accessed June 4, 2009).

Memorial Record of the Northern Peninsula of Michigan. Chicago: Lewis, 1895.

"Mrs. Garrity Dies, Aged 80." *Alpena Evening News*, December 30, 1912.

National Archives, Record Group 26, Entry 82, 83.

Nelson, Donald. "First Woman Lightkeeper on the Keweenaw Peninsula." *Lighthouse Digest*, March 2002.

Ohio Department of Natural Resources. "Marblehead Lighthouse." *Ohio State Parks.* http://www.dnr.state.oh.us/parks/magazinehome/mag1998fallwin/marbleheadfw1998/ tabid/393/default.aspx (accessed April 12, 2009).

Ontonagon Herald, February 12, 1893.

Penrod, John, and the Great Lakes Shipwreck Historical Society. *Whitefish Point Light Station: Michigan's Most Famous Lighthouse.* Berrien Center, MI: Penrod/Hiawatha, 1998.

Pepper, Terry. "Big Bay Point Lighthouse: The Story of William H. Pryor." *Seeing the Light: Lighthouses of the Western Great Lakes.* http://www.terrypepper.com/lights/superior/bigbay/priorstory.htm (accessed February 22, 2007).

Pepper, Terry. "Bois Blanc Lighthouse." *Seeing the Light: Lighthouses of the Western Great Lakes.* http://www.terrypepper.com/lights/huron/boisblanc/index.htm (accessed February 22, 2007).

Pepper, Terry. "Eagle Harbor Range Lights." *Seeing the Light: Lighthouses of the Western Great Lakes.* http://www.terrypepper.com/lights/superior/eaglerange/eaglerange.htm (accessed February 22, 2007).

Pepper, Terry. "Gull Rock Lighthouse." *Seeing the Light: Lighthouses of the Western Great Lakes.* http://www.terrypepper.com/lights/superior/gull-rock/index.htm (accessed February 22, 2007).

Pepper, Terry. "Marquette Harbor Lighthouse." *Seeing the Light: Lighthouses of the Western Great Lakes.* http://www.terrypepper.com/lights/superior/marquette/marquette.htm (accessed February 22, 2007).

Pepper, Terry. "Menagerie Island Lighthouse." *Seeing the Light: Lighthouses of the Western Great Lakes.* http://www.terrypepper.com/lights/superior/menagerie/index.htm (accessed February 22, 2007).

Pepper, Terry. "New Presque Isle Lighthouse." *Seeing the Light: Lighthouses of the*

Western Great Lakes. http://www.terrypepper.com/lights/huron/newpresqisl/
index.htm (accessed February 22, 2007).

Pepper, Terry. "Saginaw Bay Lighthouse." *Seeing the Light: Lighthouses of the Western Great Lakes.* http://www.terrypepper.com/lights/huron/saginaw-bay/index
.htm (accessed February 22, 2007).

Planisek, Sandra L. *Reliving Lighthouse Memories: 1930s–1970s.* Mackinaw City,
MI: Great Lakes Lighthouse Keepers Association, 2004.

Pleasonton, Stephen. *Instructions to the Keepers of Light-Houses within the United States.* Washington, DC: Government Printing Office, 1835.

Presque Isle County Advance, June 20, 1889.

Rezmer, Joan Totten Musinski, ed. *Women of Bay County: 1809–1980.* Bay City,
MI: Museum of the Great Lakes, 1980.

Saffron, Harold, and Linda Saffron. "Leelanau County MI Archives Photo
Tombstone: Sheridan, Julia Moore and Robert R." *USGen Web Archives.*
http://files.usgwarchives.net/mi/leelanau/photos/tombstones/southmani
touisla/sheridan135687gp h.txt (accessed January 8, 2009).

"Seacoast Women." *Seacoast New Hampshire and South Coast Maine.* http://
www.seacoastnh.com/poems/celia2.html (accessed January 25, 2009).

Shanley, Robert L., Sr. Unpublished manuscript on Anastasia Truckey, in the
possession of Chris Shanley-Dillman, Ontonagon, MI, October 30, 2001.

Shelton-Roberts, Cheryl, and Bruce Roberts. *Lighthouse Families.* Birmingham,
AL: Crane Hill, 1997.

St. Joseph's Lighthouse. Unpublished manuscript, in the collection of the Maud
Preston Palenske Memorial Library, St. Joseph, MI, undated.

St. Joseph Traveler Herald, April 2, 1881.

Stonehouse, Frederick. *Women and the Lakes: Untold Great Lakes Maritime Tales.*
Gwinn, MI: Avery Color Studios, 2001.

Stonehouse, Frederick. *Women and the Lakes II: More Untold Great Lakes Maritime Tales.* Gwinn, MI: Avery Color Studios, 2005.

Stratton, Richard. Unpublished manuscript on Mary Terry and Mrs. Peter Peterson, in the collection of the Delta County Historical Society, Escanaba, MI,
undated.

Tag, Phyllis L., and Thomas A Tag. *The Lighthouse Keepers of Lake Erie, Including Detroit River.* Dayton, OH: Great Lakes Lighthouse Research, 1998.

Traverse City Eagle-Herald, March 21, 1878.

U.S. Federal Census. Bay de Noc Township, Delta County, MI, 1900.

U.S. Federal Census. Detroit, Wayne County, MI, 1900.

U.S. Federal Census. Ecorse Township, Wayne County, MI, 1900.

U.S. Federal Census. Pipestone Township, Berrien County, MI, 1860.

U.S. Federal Census. St. Joseph, Berrien County, MI, 1880.

U.S. Light-House Establishment. *Compilation of Public Documents and Extracts
from Reports and Papers Relating to Light-Houses, Light-Vessels, and Illuminating*

Apparatus, and to Beacons, Buoys, and Fog Signals, 1789–1871. Washington, DC: Government Printing Office, 1871.

U.S. Light-House Establishment. *Rules, Regulations, and General Instructions*. Washington, DC: William A. Harris, Printer, 1858.

Vanden Bossche, Sharon Gill. "Stephen A. Warner: St. Clair, MI Lighthouse Keeper." *GenForum.* http://genforum.genealogy.com/warner/messages/3074 .html (accessed January 27, 2009).

Warnes, Kathy Covert. "The Colorful Career of Gus Gramer: Soldier, Fireman, Oarsman, and Lighthouse Person." *Lighthouse Digest*, August 2007.

Williams, Elizabeth Whitney. *A Child of the Sea; and Life among the Mormons*. St. James, MI: Henry Allen, 1905.

"Youghal." *The Commissioners of Irish Lights.* http://www.cil.ie/index.php3?area= lighthouses&LighthouseID=20 (accessed April 12, 2009).

Index

All place names are in Michigan unless otherwise indicated.

Rogers City, 66
Ross, M. B., 61
Rushmore, Maurice, 67
Rushmore, Minnie Lane, 67

Saginaw River lights, 36
Sand Point (Escanaba) light, 1, 2, 50
Sandusky, 69
Sanilac Township, 69
Shanley, Robert, 26
Sheridan, Aaron, 30, 51–52
Sheridan, George, 51–52
Sheridan, Julia, 15, 28, 30, 51–52
Sheridan, Robert, 30, 51–52
Shetterly, Henry, 36
Ship Masters Association, 43
Shook, Catherine, 6, 7, 23, 28, 30, 31, 48–49
Shook, Peter, 30, 48–49
Sinclair, John, Jr., 68
Sinclair, John, Sr., 68
South Fox Island light, 39
South Manitou Island light, 28, 51
Spanish-American War, 22, 43, 62
Squaw Point light, 64, 65
St. Clair Flats South Channel Range lights, 23, 67
St. Helena Island, 53
St. Joseph, 61
St. Joseph light, 19, 36, 61
St. Joseph Traveler Herald, 61
Stevens, M. A., 26
Stevens, William, 26
Stonehouse, Frederick, 50
Strang, James Jesse, 53, 54

Terry, John, 50
Terry, Mary, 1, 2, 50–51
Thomas, Hannah, 5
Thomas, John, 5
Thunder Bay Island light, 68
Traverse City, 54
Traverse City Eagle-Herald, 52

Truckey, Anastasia (Eliza), 21, 26, 49–50
Truckey, Nelson, 21, 26, 49–50
27th Michigan Infantry Regiment, 21
Tugboat J. M. Diver, 69

Van Benschoten, Rachel Wolcott, 6
Van Riper, Clement, 19, 30, 54
Van Riper, Elizabeth, 19, 30, 53–55
Vreeland, Mary, 19
Vreeland, Michael, 19

Walker, Herb, 69
Walker, Will, 69
Ward, Bolivar, 43
Ward, Eber, 41, 43
Ward, Emily, 41, 43
Warner, Caroline, 23
Way, George, 57
Way, Julia Brawn, 34, 36, 57
"What's My Line?," 71, 72, 82
Wheatley, Mary Ann, 20, 30, 90
Wheatley, William, 20, 30
White Lake, 70, 81
White River light, 8, 17, 21, 38, 70, 71, 74, 81
Whitefish Bay, 28
Whitefish Point light, 38
Whitehall, 86
Williams, Elizabeth Van Riper, 19–20, 23, 24, 25, 45, 47, 53–55, 90
Williams, Daniel, 55
Wolcott, Benajah, 6
Wolcott, Rachel, 6
Women Who Kept the Lights, 9
Worthylake, George, 5
Wuori, Leo, 21, 70, 71, 75, 76, 77, 78, 86–87, 89
Wyandotte, 32, 58

Youghal light (Ireland), 6
Youghans, Maria, 45

Text design by Mary H. Sexton
Typesetting by Delmastype, Ann Arbor, Michigan
Font: Goudy

Frederic W. Goudy designed Goudy Old Style in 1915.
Flexible enough for both text and display, it is one of the most
popular typefaces ever produced. Many additions to the typeface
family were created over the next several decades, including
Goudy Sans, used in this book for display elements.
   —Courtesy www.adobe.com

CPSIA information can be obtained
at www.ICGtesting.com
Printed in the USA
LVHW070549141120
671586LV00011B/58